A Stubborn
Hope

A *Stubborn Hope*

WITHOUT DISAPPOINTMENT

Jeanne DeTellis

with
Renee Meloche

NEW Missions
P.O. Box 2727
Orlando, Florida 32802

A STUBBORN HOPE

Copyright © 1996 by Jeanne DeTellis
Second printing, May 1998
Published by NEW Missions
P.O. Box 2727
Orlando, Florida 32802

Printed in the United States of America.

Contents

Chapter

Dedication

This book is dedicated to my mother, Anna DeMarco DiPietro, who was born to Italian immigrants on July 22, 1920, in Boston, Massachusetts.

At 12 years of age, my mother fell from an outside iron staircase, suffering internal injuries. A state   my mother she was going to take her to a su   rest; instead, she was placed in a sanitarium f   was separated from her family, and becaus   tance, there were few visits. At the sanit   began her search and cried out to know a li

Two years later, my Roman Catholic g   an apartment from a born-again Christian la   lady encouraged my grandmother to send my   with her at the Boston Christian Assemb   accepted Christ. Soon, my grandmother, gran   aunts and uncles came to the Lord.

At 29 years of age, my mother had   dent. She fell down a full flight of stairs i   remember throughout my childhood tha   God for her health. My father supported   her on her bad days. One day at a time, my mother   God and found His grace sufficient.

My mother turned her own personal need into an enor   mous capacity to care for others. My earliest memories are of her caring for a crippled, bedridden woman. Now, at the age of 78, she is still actively ministering to people. Her prayer list is unending.

Mom's stubborn hope in God is without disappointment.

Introduction

It was a quiet morning as I strolled along the ocean shore. The sun was peeping from the earth. It was the beginning of a new dawn. Far in the distance, I noticed a sea gull dropping down, then skimming along the water's surface.

It was hard to believe it had been 13 years since George and I first arrived in this poor and desolate country of Haiti—a country the textbooks said was beyond hope. Now, after the ravages of a November storm that left many dead, the Haitians had quietly begun picking up the pieces of their lives. Through generous donations and volunteers, reconstruction was taking place.

We also received some unexpected blessings from the tragedy. The mud had dried and cracked, enabling the grass to reappear—richer, thicker and prettier than ever. But it was the farmers who benefited the most, as the new top soil now covered the plain, nourishing and fertilizing their gardens.

The storm was a fitting paradox to one of life's great lessons. In every storm that comes our way, we have the opportunity to allow our roots to grow deeper in God, yielding even greater fruit in our lives. The greater the storm, the deeper our roots can grow to make a stronger tree.

I thought over the storms in my own life. With them came an increasing awareness that it was my own sufferings that ultimately helped me to bond with the very people God had called me to serve. As I leaned on Him to help me walk through those valleys and "keep-a-going," as my grandmother used to say, God was able to use me more effectively. And in the end, as I learned to put my trust in His unfailing love, I found a hope that would never disappoint.

As I watched the waves cascading in, one at a time, my mind replayed a hundred memories, back to my early struggles, back to my Italian roots and my unexpected entrance into another world.

Chapter 1

An Unroyal Name

Ipushed my food around my plate, wishing to escape the loud chatter of my family. They were gathered at my grandmother's table after church, trying to make our guest, a visiting pastor, feel comfortable. Being Italians, we were a close-knit family who all lived within a few miles of each other in Cambridge, Massachusetts.

I glanced at my older sister Elizabeth, sitting next to me. At 7 years old, she was definitely the beauty of the family. Tall, slender and more fair-skinned than I, she had long, ash-brown hair and brown eyes that were a shade lighter than mine. In contrast, I looked frail and underweight. Even though Mom had rolled my hair in banana curls that morning for church, I already knew I could never compete with Elizabeth.

My mother—a petite woman with blue-gray eyes whose parents had immigrated from Italy—seemed to enjoy the popularity of her oldest daughter. Raised in a tough, struggling environment, she had suffered a serious brain concussion—leaving her with a challenge to regain her health. And since Mom was a borderline anemic and a mother with two little girls, we didn't go out very much, so Elizabeth and I had no one but each other to entertain us. Although I was two years younger, I tagged along with Elizabeth and her friends whenever she'd let me.

I wiggled in my seat, impatient to go outside and play.

The adult conversation wasn't very interesting for a 5-year-old.

Then, as my grandmother whisked away our dishes and brought out Italian cookies, the conversation shifted. When Mom started to recall the details surrounding my birth, she suddenly had my attention.

"I couldn't believe I was pregnant so soon after Elizabeth," she began, shaking her head. "Then, I was so sure it would be a boy, I called the baby Robert the whole time I was pregnant."

Drawing a deep dramatic breath, Mom's eyes sparkled with amusement as she told about my delivery. "You can imagine my shock when he turned out to be a she!"

As my family chuckled, I fixed my eyes on a spot in front of me, thinking how disappointed my parents must have been.

"I didn't even have a name for her," Mom continued. "So I said to the doctor, whose wife just had a baby girl, 'Whatever you named your baby, that's what I'll name mine.' "

Slumping down in my chair, I stared at my lap. I knew Mom would never intend to hurt me in any way, but her words seemed to penetrate me like a knife. I understood two things: I was an unplanned pregnancy, and I was supposed to be a boy. And instead of a royal name like my mother Anne, my father Charles, or my older sister Elizabeth, I was named Jeanne, after the doctor's baby.

When my mother explained how she had grown to love me as a baby, I was no longer listening. Instead, the story of my birth seemed to control me: I simply wasn't supposed to have happened.

Suddenly, I wanted to disappear. Evaporate.

A deep resolve formed inside me: Since I wasn't supposed to be born, I would have to work harder to prove to others and myself that I could still amount to something.

❧   ❧   ❧   ❧   ❧

Despite the story of my birth, I had a very nurtured childhood, with parents who had a strong marriage and loved the Lord. We lived in a modest but clean five-room apartment, only a mile from my grandmother's house where I had been born. Mom opened her home constantly to missionaries and evangelists who visited our large independent Italian Pentecostal Church. Then, after our typical Italian dinner of spaghetti and meatballs, we always had a time of prayer.

Dad was a gentle, mild man who grew up on a farm near Boston. After he and my mother married, he opened an electro-plating business in the city—working with metals and chemicals. But his heart ached for the children in the city who had never experienced country living. Eventually his mother gave him part of her farmland and he started a Christian summer camp named Camp Woodhaven. Since the state owned most of the land in the area, open country surrounded the camp. In the summer we conducted meetings for people from all over the Boston area.

Not only were my parents godly examples, but both my grandmothers were bold in their faith, sharing Jesus with anyone who listened. I grew especially close to my maternal grandmother, who was there at my birth and had reassured my mother that there was nothing wrong with me. She lived near the school I attended, and I visited her every day at lunch or after school. I can still remember the huge Bible with the big Italian print laying on the kitchen table.

Although Massachusetts Institute of Technology (MIT) and Harvard University were nearby, I lived a very sheltered and narrow existence. But because of my parents' strong Christian faith and our close-knit family, I was fairly happy, even though I still battled the insecurity of being the second child and the stories surrounding my birth.

Despite the godly examples I had within my family, however, I didn't make the decision to follow Jesus right away—nor did I take it lightly. Even when I was very small, I still remember hearing my mother singing while she washed the dishes: "I'd rather have Jesus than silver or gold, I'd rather have Him than riches untold…."

Soon I was pulling on her dress: "Mommy, why can't you have both?"

Mom gazed down at me and smiled. "Once you know Jesus and give Him your life, you won't want the silver and gold."

I thought about that—hard. Even at a young age, I realized that if I chose Jesus, I would have to give up everything—and I still had a whole world to conquer to prove myself. But I also knew that no matter how much I achieved or how many possessions I accumulated, Mom and Dad would never really be pleased with me until I surrendered my life to Jesus.

During my elementary school years, my parents sometimes drove us an hour away to Zion Bible Institute where special conferences were held for the public. In front of the school was an open Bible made out of stone. Engraved in large letters was the verse from Matthew 16:26: "For what is a man profited, if he shall gain the whole world, and lose his own soul?"

Once again the question presented itself: Would I go out and try to become powerful and rich or give my all to Christ? Here I was on our school's honor roll, taking piano and accordion lessons, and doing whatever else I could to earn the approval of others. What would happen if I really lived my life to please Jesus?

My self-centered existence was not bringing me any real happiness. I was excelling, but I was still the brunt of many Italian jokes which made me feel insecure, especially since I never felt I should have been born to begin with. More and more, I only felt comfortable in my Italian Pentecostal church and within my extended family.

Often, I shared my struggles with my maternal grand-mother, who always encouraged me. Speaking with her thick Italian accent, she told me over and over again: "Keep-a-going, Jinuzia. Keep-a-going." In the years to come, I would often remind myself of that admonition.

When I was 10 years old, my mother became pregnant again. This time she was ecstatic. She had another girl and named her Karen. My baby sister had a light complexion and a round face. How I loved changing her diapers and rocking her.

Soon after Karen was born, my Sunday school teacher gave us a lesson on salvation. Afterwards, she said, "If you want to accept the Lord today, let me know."

After the other seven girls had left, I approached my teacher, telling her I wanted to ask Jesus into my heart.

"There really isn't time now, dear," she explained, snatching her purse and Bible off a table. "I need to have a quick lunch and then visit another church. Maybe we can do it another Sunday."

As disappointment clouded my face, I nodded and walked out the door. Then I reminded myself of my teacher's words. Maybe another Sunday....

Yet, as the year slipped by, my teacher must have forgotten. We never did pray together.

The following year I had a new teacher. She was a single Italian about 30 years old with dark, shining eyes. On a frosty February day after church, she invited us to her home for lunch. Feeling all grown up in my pump shoes and nylon stockings, I walked the short distance to the railroad station with several other girls, then took a train to her small, modest home.

Soon we were eating an Italian meal of spaghetti and meatballs. Just as I anticipated spending the afternoon playing games and relaxing, she announced, "We're going to have church now in the living room."

What a terrible trick, I thought. As I scanned the faces of the other girls, I could tell they felt the same way.

While our teacher played the piano, we gathered around her, singing a few hymns. Then she had us get on our knees while she prayed for us.

What happened next was a surprise. Suddenly, the words of the Scripture emblazoned in stone at Zion Bible Institute buzzed around my head: "For what is a man profited, if he shall gain the whole world, and lose his own soul?"

Next, the song that my mother used to sing echoed and repeated in my mind: "I'd rather have Jesus than silver or gold...." Up until now, I had wanted to be a big success in every way and to work hard—displaying my trophies for all the world to see. But now, for the first time that I could remember, I actually wanted Jesus more than the silver or gold or status.

Slowly, quietly, the tears slid down my cheeks as a quiet hush filled the room. Then, as I asked Jesus to come into my heart, I felt His overwhelming, unconditional love for me. For the first time, I realized I didn't have to do anything to earn His love and acceptance: I already had it. My heart also burned with an intense desire to serve Him and to become a missionary. From then on, I knew my life would be motivated by that one thing.

But could God really use me? I wondered. A short, ordinary-looking girl with a common name who was supposed to be a boy? Maybe, though, because I was an Italian and was sure I wouldn't be getting married, I could start an orphanage in Italy. Maybe—just maybe—God would find a place for me after all.

Little did I realize that God's plans for me would be far different than my own. Even the rejection I had felt as a child would be important in developing the compassion and sensitivity I would need to fulfill His purposes for my life.

Chapter 2

I Surrender All

I sat riveted to my seat as the young Bible school student bounded to the pulpit, greeting us with a big welcoming smile that displayed strong white teeth. His dark hair looked as though it had been slicked back by Vitalis, and he was sharp and slim in his navy-blue suit. His warm brown eyes sparkled with humor and intelligence. He was an Italian named George DeTellis, and I soon discovered that he was very popular with the young women.

Yet, since I was only 13 and George was seven years older than me, I was definitely not interested. Instead, it was his zeal and intense love for God that impressed me.

Soon my heart was being challenged by George's sermon, which admonished us to be willing to go into Christian service. However, I wondered if God could really use me. Plagued by doubt, my mind flashed back to the conversation I had with my eighth-grade home room teacher only weeks earlier:

> *"What sort of education did your parents have?" she asked, peering at me across her desk through thick glasses.*
> *"My father came from a large family. He had to leave school to work on the farm. My mother also came from a large family. She felt she had to help and went to work before she finished high school."*

"Then I don't think you're college
material, dear. Don't bother taking any of
the more difficult subjects to prepare for it."
        Returning to my seat, I felt alone and
miserable.

The words of my teacher had left me terribly disheart-
ened. I stayed on the honor roll, but now I was trying to
excel in school for a different reason: I wanted to better
equip myself to serve God on the mission field. Already, I
was studying the Italian language, teaching Sunday school
to 6-year-old Italian immigrants at a small church, and playing the piano for them.

I had also made a commitment to God, promising to
tell someone about Jesus every day. Just in case I got behind,
I stayed up late at night scanning the telephone directory for
names. Starting with the "A's," I wrote letters to people I had
never met telling them about Jesus. Along with the letter, I
enclosed a Christian tract, using my spare money to buy
them. When I finally got tired of writing, I went from house
to house stuffing tracts into people's mailboxes. But soon
the mailman found out about it, and told my mother it was
against the law.

Although I may have been trying to win God's
approval, I had a burning, overwhelming desire to be used
by Him. Besides, I knew that if I gained the approval of
man, I would get a few minutes of applause, but that if I did
things for God, I would be rewarded for eternity.

So great was my desire to please God that during the
summer, while helping out at vacation Bible school, I got
down on my knees and cried out to God, begging Him to use
me. I didn't care what I did. I wanted to do something for
God.

Just then, one of our leaders peeked her head in the
door. "Don't worry, honey," she responded, obviously

overhearing me. "You don't have to pray that prayer anymore. There's plenty for you to do."

Yet, I wasn't so sure. The details of my birth and the words of my teacher still made me feel so inadequate: I wasn't supposed to be born. I was supposed to be a boy. I wasn't college material. And now I had become a short and chubby teenage girl who didn't have a clue how God could use her. *Did God have a plan for me anyway?* I wondered.

Yet, now as George DeTellis asked those who wanted to serve God in full-time Christian service to come forward, my heart pounded. As we opened our hymnals and sang the words to "I Surrender All," I slid out of my pew and went forward.

When the music was over, I found myself standing alone, willing and waiting—waiting for the day when God might somehow use me on the mission field. George looked at me, his eyes shining with approval. Little did I know how great a part he would play in the plans God had for me.

Chapter 3

A New Direction

I lugged my heavy accordion down the street as George DeTellis walked beside me, carrying the speaker system. Two years had passed since George had first spoken at our church, and now he was back for the summer, leading our youth ministry. Each week, we went to the Boston Common where we witnessed and had open-air meetings.

Although I still lacked self-confidence, I had dieted down to an acceptable weight and was fairly attractive. Still, I had only two friends in the large high school where I attended—both of them Baptists. I don't remember anyone else being an Italian Pentecostal except my sister Elizabeth, and she wasn't about to let anyone find out. Since I didn't have much of a social life, I channeled my energy and drive into practical ways of helping a pioneer church in East Boston—cleaning, teaching, and playing the piano and accordion.

As George and I headed towards the park, he studied me intently, asking what I wanted to do with my life. Immediately, I told him I wanted to be a missionary. George gave me a long, contemplative look. He explained that when he was converted four years earlier—the same year I had been—he had also felt called to the mission field, specifically South America.

∞ ∞ ∞ ∞ ∞

The weeks flew by as George and I spent lots of time together in ministry. Then, towards the end of the summer, he visited me at my home. Sitting together in the living room, he read some romantic story in the Bible. It was then that I realized something was up.

When he finished, he reached for my hand. "I love you," he whispered.

My heart beat out of control as I sat there surprised, yet delighted.

"Do you love me?" he asked.

"Yes!" I told him quickly.

George went into the kitchen to talk with my parents, leaving me to wonder about God's plan for my future. Until now, I had always thought I was going to be a single missionary. Did God have other plans for my life after all?

For the rest of the summer, George and I double-dated with my sister Elizabeth, who was dating a man named Peter. The two of them planned to be married in a year, after she had graduated from high school.

Soon it was time for George to attend Central Bible College in Springfield, Missouri, 1,500 miles away. Our romance blossomed long-distance as he completed his education and received his B.A. degree. After graduating, George returned to the Boston area and started a church under the Assemblies of God umbrella, renting a hall on the second floor of the town theater. Every Saturday night I helped him clean up cigarettes and beer bottles, left over from the bingo games. Since George had no money for a vehicle, my dad let him borrow his to pick up children for Sunday school. Meanwhile, I became the piano player, Sunday school teacher, and secretary. And, since I had a part-time job as a typist, I was given permission to do the church bulletin each week on the company steno machine.

As soon as I graduated from high school at 17, I found full-time work as a secretary while waiting until I was 18 to

marry, according to my parents' wishes. To prepare myself
for Christian service, I still wanted to attend college. I was
on the honor roll throughout high school and had won
awards for both my secretarial and Italian language skills,
but I still had nagging doubts that I wasn't college material.

Nevertheless, I gathered my courage and walked into
Suffolk University in Boston and applied. Much to my
astonishment, I was accepted. As I continued working, I
attended school part-time, and discovered I was able to han-
dle the course work after all.

On June 25, 1960—I had turned 18 three weeks earlier—we were married in true Italian style: Lots of food and
more than 350 people in attendance. After a two-week hon-
eymoon in which we ended up assisting nightly revival services in Canada, we returned home.

Surprisingly, George and I didn't head for the mission
field like I had thought. Instead, we took the $4,000 we had
received for our wedding and bought a large three-story
home in Medford, Massachusetts—just eight miles from
Cambridge—and began a church. Standing near the center
of town, the home, which once belonged to the mayor, had
a spacious yard filled with cherry blossom trees, rose bushes
and a sunken-tile bird bath. It even had a large barn which
we planned to use for special youth programs.

A few months after the purchase, one of George's pastor friends admonished us: "In a few years, you're going to
regret you bought this home in the church's name. When
you leave you'll have nothing for your family."

I thought seriously about what our friend said when I
discovered shortly afterwards that I was pregnant. Then I
remembered the Scripture from Matthew 6:33: "But seek
first His kingdom and His righteousness; and all these things
shall be added to you" (NAS). Somehow, George and I
knew, when the time came for us to leave, God would take
care of us.

We lived on the second floor of the house, and church was held downstairs in a spacious double room on the first floor. We threw ourselves into the ministry, never bothering to take a day off. We thrived in our new environment. George loved to see people nurtured in the Word of God as he preached each Sunday, and I quickly became comfortable in my role as a pastor's wife, supporting George wherever possible. Besides entertaining frequently and being the church secretary and piano player, I tried to make each woman feel special without showing favoritism. At the same time, I never allowed myself to share any of my personal problems. Although I didn't have intimate friendships as a result, I was experiencing a growing bond with this church we were pioneering, breaking outside of my closed Italian existence.

On June 11—almost a year after we married, George and I became the proud parents of a baby boy, naming him George, Jr. He was a typical Italian baby with olive skin and lots of black hair.

Then, when George, Jr. was only 3 months old, I became pregnant again. This time, in my third month, I had a miscarriage. Since I had already carried one child to term and was young and healthy, I felt it would simply be an isolated incident.

The following summer, George ran my father's camp—Camp Woodhaven—for six weeks while I helped with the hospitality and accounting work. Although there were fun times of swimming and baseball, most people came with a deep hunger to know God. We had music and speakers from all over New England, and many people were saved. Once, after the children were put to bed at night, the neighbors called the police because our campers were still praying at 11:00, creating a disturbance.

As we concentrated all our efforts on our church and summer camp, the mission call on our lives slowly faded from view. Not only did we not have a missions program, but the word "missions" rarely came to our lips. Instead, our call to missions was buried somewhere beneath our activity, waiting for the right time to come alive again. Yet, even in our present circumstances, God was preparing us. We lived on a meager salary of $25 a week, and I was learning to depend on His provision and be creative with what we were given. Every Sunday, one of my mother's friends filled our refrigerator freezer with frozen meat. This helped tremendously. Also, we were able to keep whatever government commodities were left over after camp: flour, oatmeal, peanut butter, oil, beans, and rice. Slowly, God was teaching me a new contentment that would help me cope with much more difficult living situations in the future.

When George, Jr. was 13 months old, I discovered I was pregnant again. It was then that the doctors informed me that George and I had blood types that weren't compatible: I was RH negative, and he was RH positive.

On February 12—just a year and a half after George, Jr. was born—they induced labor when I was eight months pregnant. We named our second baby boy Charles after my father. Although he was put in intensive care and had to have two blood exchanges at birth, he was soon in stable condition.

I was able to take Charlie home after two weeks. But before I left, I was warned that with each pregnancy, the risks would increase, for I would continue to build up more and more antibodies to fight and attack my husband's blood.

Shortly after Charlie's birth, I suffered another miscarriage when I was a few months along. Then, when George, Jr. and Charlie were 4- and 2-years old, I gave birth to our first daughter, Mary Ann, named after both of her grandmothers, on December 28. She was a fair-skinned, light-haired child. Like Charlie, she was taken when I was eight months pregnant and immediately given two blood exchanges.

After four years, our church was flourishing so well that we bought a bigger facility, allowing us to rent out part of our first home to boarders and use the money to help pay off our mortgage. At the same time, George bought a piece of land next to the expressway. Since it was in a prime location, he dreamed of eventually building a new facility there, enabling us to extend our reach into the greater community.

Meanwhile, we were still receiving a salary of $25 a week. Finally, our church elders convinced us to accept an increase to $50 a week. Even that didn't satisfy our leadership. They encouraged us to sell one of our properties to raise our salary higher so we wouldn't have to live on leftovers and wear hand-me-down clothes.

Although we refused to sell, the suggestion was tempting. For now, just three and a half months after Mary Ann was born, I discovered we would soon have another mouth to feed.

Chapter 4

His Grace is Sufficient

I placed my hand on my swollen belly, feeling the baby's movements in my womb. How I looked forward to the birth of this little one. And because of the many x-rays I received during this pregnancy, I already knew I was carrying a girl.

Somehow spring had slipped away, and we were spending the summer living in tents at Camp Woodhaven. Besides my family responsibilities, I played the piano and was in charge of the kitchen, which meant planning and shopping for all the meals. At night, I entertained whatever guest speaker was there.

One of our guests finally admonished me: "You're working too hard. Your body's going to break down."

I gave a little laugh and shrugged off the warning. I was strong, healthy, and zealous for God. Besides, I loved the challenge of being so busy. Unfortunately, it would take a grave illness before I finally took the pastor's advice seriously.

By the time I was almost eight months pregnant, I had had three inter-uterine blood transfusions because my baby's blood was being destroyed. To perform this procedure, doctors had to x-ray the position of my baby and insert a needle into her stomach. If they missed, the baby would die. Fortunately, the transfusions had been successful.

The doctors had warned me that my risks would increase with each pregnancy, but I knew I would have this baby. Although I still required one more blood transfusion, I was so close to delivery time that I was no longer concerned. I had already named her Elizabeth Jean, after my sister Elizabeth. We would nickname her Betty Jean, rounding out our family to two girls and two boys. Perfect.

On October 27, when I was eight months pregnant, I went to Boston Hospital for my fourth inter-uterine blood transfusion. After an apparently successful procedure, I let myself relax as I realized my baby's birth was almost a certainty now.

That evening, I set my hair in rollers, preparing to look as nice as possible for my return home the following morning. Afterwards, I reached for my Bible on the table next to me and randomly opened it. Immediately, a verse from Matthew 26:39 seemed to leap off the page: "…if it is possible, may this cup be taken from me. Yet not as I will, but as you will" (NIV).

A twinge of apprehension shot through me as I placed my hand on my stomach and waited in tense silence, holding my breath. As the minutes ticked by, I prayed for some sign of life. But there was nothing. Not even a flutter.

My stomach knotted as my heart sank. I was certain my baby girl had died.

A few tears escaped down my cheeks as my eyes scanned my small room. It was cold. Dark. For a moment, time seemed to stop. Unknown voices from the hallway grew fainter until they finally went quiet altogether. Afterwards, a heavy silence settled over the place.

My eyes puffed and reddened as I pulled the blanket up to my neck. Then, rolling over in the darkness, I wrapped my arms tightly around my baby. Yet, in this terrible hour, I suddenly knew I wasn't alone.

Blinking back tears, I opened my eyes, sensing Jesus' healing presence in that small, sterile room. Whatever the outcome, I knew He would be with me—loving me, comforting me, holding me. As I pictured myself in His arms, I was finally able to drift off into a deep, peaceful sleep.

Then, just before midnight, I jolted awake and threw off my covers. Staring at my sheet, I let out an audible gasp: I was surrounded by a pool of blue water. Apparently my water had broken, but why was it blue? Then I remembered: Just before they took the x-ray, they had dyed my water in order to see my baby's position more clearly.

I called a nurse, and they whisked me to the labor room. The contractions began soon afterwards, but I put off calling George, feeling he could use a good night's sleep, especially with three little ones at home. Instead, I focused all my energy into praying that my baby girl might possibly be alive.

Four hours later, a doctor and nurse entered my room. Just before dawn, I delivered Betty Jean, catching a glimpse of her black hair as the doctor whisked her away.

Then I heard the noise: *Plop!*

Aware that a bucket of water lay at the foot of my bed, I recoiled in horror. My precious baby girl had just been dropped into it, like a rag doll being thrown away. At that moment the ache in my soul reached deeper than ever before. I felt depleted. Empty.

"Your baby's dead," the nurse responded with a detached, professional gaze.

My heart wrenched at her words. Obviously, the needle that had been inserted at the time of the inter-uterine blood transfusion had hit Betty Jean in the wrong place and killed her.

Mustering my courage, I lifted my chin and asked, "Can I sing a song?"

"Sure. Whatever you want."

In a halting voice, I sang out: "Keep praising the Lord when the skies above are gray, Keep praising the Lord for the answer's on the way. Do not despair, for the Lord will answer prayer, For those who endure the victory is sure, Keep praising the Lord..." Over and over, I repeated the words until they became like a balm of healing ointment to my broken heart.

Elizabeth Jean was born on my sister Elizabeth's birthday. The next day she was buried in the family cemetery.

Over the next several weeks, I focused my eyes on Jesus, allowing Him to continue to comfort me in my sorrow. Whenever I felt overcome with grief and disappointment, I could feel Him—the God of all hope and of all love—pick me up and carry me, giving me the grace and strength to move on.

I had little time to grieve. Soon after my baby's death, George decided to go into full-time evangelism. Although our church was thriving after six years, we turned over the keys and the deeds of the church and our home to our board members. George bought some radio equipment and air time and signed up with three radio stations, starting his own George DeTellis Evangelistic Association.

A short time later, George received a call from a church in Erie, Pennsylvania. The congregation was without leadership and wondered if George would serve as an interim pastor until they found someone. George decided to accept the offer, and we packed up our children and drove the 1,000 miles to Erie.

In January, two and a half months after Betty Jean's death, we arrived in Erie where we stayed in a new brick ranch home that the church had provided for us. The congregation itself was older and established with 300 members who loved and treated us like royalty. It was a completely new experience from pioneering a church.

In spite of the generous $150 a week salary, 80 percent of it went to pay for George's radio broadcasts. Once again, we struggled to make ends meet.

After a fruitful three months in Pennsylvania, our interim ended, and, despite the pleas from the congregation for us to stay permanently, we decided we should leave. George felt called to full-time evangelism.

Soon my family and I were living in a white two-story summer house near Camp Woodhaven, which my parents owned. It had three bedrooms and a large living room. Off of the kitchen was a family room that led out to a deck overlooking a rolling green meadow. My dad helped us fix up the place, making it livable for the approaching New England winter. Eventually, he even built a fieldstone fireplace that filled the entire living room wall. Mom also pitched in, buying us expensive wallpaper, red carpeting, and fine Victorian furniture.

The house was very spacious, more than adequate for my growing family. George, Jr., who was 6 years old, had become an easygoing, responsible child. Although he had attended three different kindergartens already, he had made the adjustments without any problem. My husband had instilled a strong work ethic in George, Jr., and he was responding by becoming a diligent worker, able to vacuum the entire house for me.

Charlie, now 4-years-old, was much quieter than George, Jr., content to follow his older brother wherever he went. Mary Ann was also a quiet 2-year-old with soft, curly-blond hair. Unfortunately, she often had to play by herself since no girls her age were nearby, and her brothers didn't seem to enjoy her tagging along with them.

Despite the tranquil setting, and as grateful as I was to my parents for letting us live there, I was terribly lonely. George was now traveling throughout the East Coast, holding revival meetings. Although I knew God was using him powerfully during these times, he was rarely home. That meant I was left to take care of our three children by myself without a car and with the nearest store ten miles away. My parents were supportive, and did what they could to help out, but it was still difficult.

Once again, I struggled to put food on the table, living off whatever was left over from the offerings that George received each week. Somehow this wasn't what I pictured when I had asked God to use me. I always loved supporting my husband in the ministry, but now I wondered what was I doing way out in no man's land with only the trees and squirrels to talk to.

One Sunday morning we visited a church just ten miles from our home. Church was held in a dilapidated, wooden, three-story Salvation Army building, located in the downtown area of the city. Eight elderly people joined us in a large room as we sat together on broken folding chairs. Meanwhile, our children attended Sunday school in the basement. When the service was over, Mary Ann, who was 2 years old and wearing a white lace pinafore dress with pink tights, was completely black from the soot.

I knew George was also tired of the constant travel and separation between us, but I was not prepared for our next step. When the pastor of the church announced he was leaving, George decided to take his place.

I was far from happy about this decision. The church was situated in Worcester, a former industrial city on a major route to Boston in a poor neighborhood. The outside of the building had been partially painted three times so that gray, green, and barn-red paint showed through simultaneously. Kids hung out on the street corners, and many of the families wrestled with alcoholism and divorce. Even though a hospital was located next to us and offered easy, free parking, I knew that many people would not consider attending the church because of its location.

Why, I wondered, *would George want to take a struggling ministry like this when we could have stayed on at the church in Erie, Pennsylvania? Or why didn't we return to the church we pioneered in Medford where we were already loved and established?*

Despite my arguments, George saw this as a base from which he could reach out in evangelism. Reluctantly, I agreed as he took over as their pastor. At least it gave us a steady salary again, even if it was only $50 a week.

During the first month we were there, George cleaned the church room by room, filling several truckloads of rubbish. I did my best to support him by playing the piano and inviting people who needed encouragement to our home each week. And even though the more well-to-do didn't want to be associated with our church, they began attending Bible studies in our home.

It was still a struggle for me, however. Even though our congregation continued growing with good, dedicated people, I realized I was having a hard time bonding. Often, I was on my knees before the Lord, confessing my inability to feel a deep love for the people and for this ministry.

George and I had been married and in the ministry for seven years. Although I was only 25 years old and was committed to supporting my husband in any capacity, I secretly wished for some other way for us to serve God together.

Soon, however, my mind shifted to another concern. The following summer, less than a year after losing my baby girl, Betty Jean, I became pregnant again. The members of our congregation knew of my past difficulties and offered advice and prayers. Sometimes their words stung. For example, one Sunday a tall, well-meaning Swedish woman approached me after church. Pointing her finger at my stomach, she explained, "If you had had faith, you wouldn't have lost those other children."

Maybe she was right, I decided. So, while she and others prayed and fasted for me, I took positive action and did my best to become Saint Jeanne. Spending every possible moment I could in prayer and Bible reading, I focused my thoughts on believing, believing, and believing for this baby.

When I drove, I sang songs of faith. When I did the dishes, I proclaimed that Jesus was my deliverer and my healer. I was determined not to lose another baby because of my lack of faith.

Then, in my sixth month, after I had had two inter-uterine blood transfusions, the Chief of Staff at the Boston Hospital for Women—the same doctor who had delivered each of my children—approached me. I'm sorry," he explained, "but your baby is dead."

"My baby is not dead," I responded emphatically. I wasn't going to listen to man, I decided, but was going to trust and believe God.

Soon afterwards, on New Year's Eve, a small crowd clustered in my home church in Boston which I attended during my childhood. We had gathered to bring in the New Year of 1969. During the evening, several people inquired about my baby. I explained to each of them that the doctor said the baby was dead, but I still had faith that the baby was alive.

Five weeks passed slowly as I continued to believe my baby was alive and in God's care. Finally, because my doctor felt it was becoming dangerous to keep a dead baby inside me for so long, he recommended that they induce labor.

Reluctantly, I agreed. Yet, even as I entered the hospital, I was still convinced that my baby was alive.

A few hours after delivery, however, I was faced with the cold reality of my situation: My baby boy really was dead.

Before I had a chance to say goodbye, a nurse whisked him away without my ever seeing him.

The next day, I left the hospital in a black rayon maternity dress that I had borrowed from my sister Elizabeth— unfortunately well-suited for the occasion. Even though I felt confused and a little foolish, I felt no anger or questioning towards God. Once again, His peace settled over me like a warm blanket. And if I was a fool, I surmised, at least I was a fool because I loved God and had wanted my faith to please Him. Now, however, I knew that my faith would have to operate in the dark. Perhaps some day I would see His perspective on what was accomplished by "every grain of wheat which falls into the earth and dies" (John 12:24). And although I didn't understand it at the time, losing my children would ultimately be something God would use as part of His plans and purposes for me—an eventual gold mine of future ministry relationships.

George and I named the baby Jonathan and buried him next to Betty Jean. Afterwards, my doctor informed me that I should never get pregnant again—it was impossible for me to have another child.

From then on, we took no chances. George, who felt I had been through enough, agreed that I should not become pregnant again.

As consumed as we were by events in our personal lives, we were aware that a supernatural wave of God was moving through America. What we didn't realize was that we were about to ride the wave all the way to the top.

Chapter 5

Riding the Wave

The room was crowded as a barefooted, long-haired man—seated on a high stool—sang and played the guitar: "Put your hand in the hand of the Man who stilled the waters. . . ." Teenagers, Vietnam veterans, and other young adults—dressed in T-shirts and patched jeans—clapped and joined in enthusiastically. Huddled in a corner with my three children, I swayed my head from side to side and sang along with them.

A few months earlier, George had returned from a visit to California where he had observed a powerful move of God among the young people. Afterwards, we fixed up the basement of our church, transforming it into the first Christian coffeehouse in New England. We called the place Charisma Coffee House.

Now, as I scanned my surroundings, I was amazed at the change that had taken place. The walls were painted sea colors, giving the room a warm, cozy feeling. Old wine barrels had been turned upside down and transformed into tables with lighted candles on top. Fishing nets were strewn from the ceiling, with colored-glass balls hanging across the place.

Every Friday night, young people flocked to our coffeehouse in search of a real relationship with Jesus. Soon churches began sending their youth leaders to our place to see what we were doing. Before long, coffeehouses were springing up all over New England.

The youth poured into our Sunday church service as well. By this time, only one elderly woman remained—a woman who recognized that this "Jesus Movement" was a sovereign move of God. I realized it too, yet I still struggled. I came from a proper Pentecostal background where wearing slacks wasn't allowed—only dresses, gloves and hats; if we weren't dressed appropriately, we were sent home. Yet, now in our Sunday services, all I saw was dirty feet, stringy long hair, and old, worn jeans.

Fortunately, my husband was wise enough to recognize that God was doing something powerful. So here I was—just like on any other Friday night—dressed in button-down jeans with my hair swooped up in pigtails. While my children played by my side, I pushed my prejudice feelings away, talking and praying with the young people until midnight or later. I knew it was important that I look past the outward appearance and see what God was doing. And it was obvious that they were children of God, and His Spirit was moving upon them.

Besides our coffeehouse, George also rented auditoriums where we held large rallies. The first time we rented an auditorium and hired a gospel music band, we had to finally close the doors because there were too many people. We took the excess crowd down the road to our own church which they packed out as well. Then, back in the auditorium, after a band played and George spoke, I played the piano as hundreds moved forward to receive Jesus, and then later into side rooms for counseling. Afterwards, George and I drove over to the church where many more were saved.

Eventually we purchased two large homes across the street from our church to provide a Christian environment for young people who were coming off of drugs. I spent considerable time preparing the menus and scheduling the cooking, making sure things ran smoothly. Mary Ann, now 6 years old, pitched in as well, bringing the women special treats or small gifts for their birthdays. Even at a young age, she had developed a sensitivity for the down-and-outer of any age.

One Sunday after church, I waited with the children as George, still handsome and charismatic as ever, counseled a 19-year-old off to the side. She lived in the community house and constantly wanted George's attention. Since I believed the girl's intentions were harmless, and I knew George was very careful whenever he counseled any of the young women, I bit my lip, trying to control my anger. Everywhere I looked, needy young people seemed to demand first place in my husband's life.

Although George was always home for dinner and wanted me with him in everything he did, the young people seemed to be invading our lives. Our conversations around the dinner table or driving home from church were centered on the ministry, allowing little time for our children to talk about their own lives. On top of that, since George never took a day off, I was left alone most of the time to care for our children, only adding to my pain.

When George finally finished his conversation with the girl, she had become my mental scapegoat. And as we headed home, resentment churned inside of me. At the first opportunity, I poured out my frustrations to my husband.

"You'll always be number one in my heart," George responded in a comforting tone.

After a long pause, I finally nodded. Even though George continued to reassure me, I was still plagued by insecurities from my childhood—insecurities that God would have to heal if I were to be free to love and minister to others.

For now, I only knew that my spiritual growth would be greatly undermined unless I dealt with my attitude. So, each Sunday as I was served communion, I confessed to God my growing resentment. However, it was a constant battle—one I seemed to be losing.

Meanwhile, two years after the Jesus Movement had begun, George felt it was time to leave the pastorate and go into full-time evangelism. Although I was thrilled for him because of the tremendous fulfillment I knew he would experience, I wondered if this was the way God would continue to use us. The mission dream had long since been buried for George and me; we didn't even have a missions program in our church and didn't invite missionaries to speak at the services. Instead, George was heavily involved in local evangelism, and I was now a pastor's wife with three children: Life had simply taken a different road for the two of us. Yet, now that my children were all in school I had a little more free time, making me long for something more. I loved being George's helpmate, I loved being a mother to my children, and yet...

One evening, George invited the vice-president of a Catholic college to dinner. Just before Father O'Halloran left, I ventured, "Do you think I could be a good pastor's wife and mother and still return to school?"

"If you have a healthy mind, you can do all three."

That was all the encouragement I needed. With George's full support, I attended school part-time, working towards an A.A. degree in secretarial studies. Forever practical, I knew God always had a need for secretaries.

Then, halfway through my second semester, I discovered distressing news.

Chapter 6

Against the Odds

Sitting cross-legged on the carpeted corridor of the college, I tried to concentrate as a wave of nausea swept over me. *It must be because they're painting one of the classrooms*, I decided.

However, the flu symptoms wouldn't go away. Finally, I drove with Cathy—one of our church teenagers—to the Boston Hospital for Women where I soon was told what I had already feared. The Chief of Staff stared at me grimly and delivered the news that I was pregnant again. Obviously, the precautions my husband and I had taken to prevent another baby hadn't worked. "There's no possibility you can have this child," the doctor explained. "I'll schedule you for an abortion in two days. You'll be back in time for your midterms."

His words rang with authority. I had the best medical advice available and saw no reason to disagree. Feeling faint and tired, I nodded my assent, then escaped from the room. As I headed towards the cafeteria for a cup of coffee, I determined that no one—except George—would ever find out about this.

Moments later, one of my mother's best friends, who was with her pregnant sister, approached me. She peered at me curiously and pointed her finger at my stomach: "You better not be pregnant again."

"Oh no," I countered quickly. "I just came here for my annual checkup."

Cutting the conversation short, I turned and pushed through the cafeteria door. Then it hit me: Not only had I just lied to this woman, but she was sure to tell my mother she saw me at this hospital—and Mom would know that I wouldn't travel an hour and a half for a physical exam. It was then that I realized I would have to let my mother in on my secret.

Driving home with Cathy, unrelenting sheets of rain battered my windshield as I felt a flood of emotions sweep over me. I thought of the baby I was about to abort, and a knot formed in the pit of my stomach—an aching, sick-at-heart feeling. Even though I told myself the decision was logical and sensible, I was plagued by guilt and shame. I pushed aside my emotions and tried not to think about the tiny life growing within me. Instead, as I blindly sped along the freeway in the torrential rains, I focused my energies on trying to make it home.

I arrived safely a short time later, and my family was all there to greet me—my husband, 11-year-old George, Jr., 9-year-old Charlie, and 7-year-old Mary Ann. How precious each one of them was. Yet, between George's ministry, my schooling, and the children's activities, we hardly enjoyed a free moment. It was obvious that having an abortion now would save us all a lot of trouble later, eliminating the pain of explaining to the children the death of their newborn brother or sister. We couldn't expect them to understand.

That evening, however, George was somber when I told him my plans. "Is there any chance the baby might live?" he asked.

"There's always a chance, but it's too small to consider."

"Oh," he responded. His voice was soft, distant.

I found his quiet response difficult. Couldn't he see that we needed to be sensible about this?

Next, I called my mother, who tried to support the doctor's decision. Placing the receiver back in the cradle, I stood there despondently. George, Jr.—who had overheard our conversation—approached me. "Mommy," he questioned, "why do you have to have an abortion?"

"Honey, try to understand. The baby is going to die anyway. I'm just going to…. " Not wanting to finish the sentence, I tried a different approach. "The problem is, the baby's blood is not compatible with mine, and it won't survive. So if we end its life now, then…"

George, Jr. looked at me stubbornly. "The other babies died by themselves. Why don't you just let this baby die naturally too?"

That was just like a youngster, I thought, *unable to see the wisdom of what I was about to do. Didn't he understand how hard it was to carry a child seven or eight months, only to have it die?* I simply couldn't go through that again.

Yet, that evening sleep escaped me as George, Jr.'s words kept playing over and over in my mind. Why did I feel so uncertain about such a logical decision? I cried out to my Heavenly Father. As I prayed, memories of my two miscarriages and the still births of Betty Jean and Jonathan came flooding back. As I thought about the pain and disappointment, I also remembered the presence of God that had been there during each delivery, comforting me.

My mind continued to linger over the past. I reflected on the grace I had received after losing each of my babies. With the memory came the realization that there was no need to take matters in my own hands during this pregnancy either. I knew that if this baby died—even late in my pregnancy—God would give me the grace to suffer the loss. For certainly, the God of all comfort would support and give me hope in the tomorrows, just as surely as He had supported me in the yesterdays.

The following morning, I told George my decision. He supported me wholeheartedly and said a prayer of blessing and protection over me. Then I called the hospital and canceled the abortion.

My doctor, however, was not happy about this recent change of heart. Feeling that my situation was hopeless and that my baby would ultimately die, he regarded my decision as irresponsible. Nevertheless, he agreed to help me as much as possible.

When I was four months pregnant, I finished my spring semester at school, and, although I had only completed one year of requirements, I decided not to continue until after my baby was born. Instead, during my pregnancy, my family and I spent the summer on Cape Cod working in evangelism.

Along with George and his evangelism team from church, I spent my days witnessing on the beaches. Mary Ann, dressed in bib overalls with her hair in two blonde pigtails, tagged along with her two older brothers, passing out announcements of our upcoming rallies and copies of our newspaper. During the night, we slept on the floors of two Methodist churches.

Once a week we held a rally in the biggest auditorium we could find. Each time, we were able to pay the bands and feed our evangelism team from the offerings we received, but we still struggled as a family to meet our own needs.

In the past, God had always faithfully provided for us, yet now the financial stress coupled with the possibility of losing my baby was almost more than I could bear. Whenever I felt the pressures mounting, I admonished myself, just as David did in the book of Psalms: "Why are you downcast, O my soul? Why so disturbed within me? Put your hope in God, for I will yet praise him, my Savior and my God" (Psalm 43:5 NIV).

When I was five months pregnant, I attended an evening rally where several people gave testimonies of the wonderful things God had done in their lives. As I listened, the Lord's peace settled on me in a real way. Even though it seemed impossible—especially in light of the doctor's grim verdict—I felt a sense of renewed hope and reassurance that this baby was going to make it.

The Lord continued to encourage me, and my faith and courage rose with a new resolve. "Lord," I whispered in response, "I trust You. And I really believe You're going to let this baby live." Afterwards, I went out and shopped for maternity clothes.

Two days later, however, my courage began to wane. The hospital had called, explaining it was necessary for me to undergo an inter-uterine blood transfusion. A wave of panic washed over me as I realized the procedure had become necessary far earlier than any of my other pregnancies. Yet, if they didn't do it now, my baby would either die or be brain-damaged because its blood had already been so adversely affected. So after preparing a big lasagna meal for the team, I left George and my three children on Cape Cod while Cathy—the same teenager who'd driven me earlier to take my pregnancy test—drove me once again to the Boston Hospital for Women.

After the two-hour procedure, I lay in the cold, cheerless hospital room, awaiting the outcome. Placing my hand on my stomach, I tensed and listened for some sign of life. One minute passed. Then another. And another. Silence. And then...

Thump! My heart leapt like a child's on Christmas morning. My baby had kicked!

A short time later, a nurse heard the heartbeat, confirming that my baby had survived the transfusion.

"Aren't you lucky that transfusion was a success?" the doctor asked later.

I shook my head. "I wasn't lucky. It was God."

By the time I was six months pregnant—after two more successful transfusions—my water broke. My neighbor, who was a nurse, told me there was little chance of the baby's survival now. As George drove me the long distance to the hospital and encouraged me to be brave, I choked back my tears as I tried to sing "His Banner Over Me Is Love."

I was placed in a ward with 21 other women, separated only by thin panels and a small curtain in front of my bed. Wrapping myself in the comfort of God's Word, I meditated on one verse in particular: "Be still, and know that I am God" (Psalm 46:10 NIV). Whenever my anxieties mounted, this verse helped me to rest and put my faith and hope securely in Him. Whatever the outcome, I realized that His presence and grace would be sufficient once again to see me through this new crisis.

For several weeks, I was on hospital bedrest while George visited when he found someone to watch our other three children. Fortunately, my parents also pitched in, helping with the children whenever they could.

Then, on September 29, when I was almost seven months along, a stabbing pain awoke me in the middle of the night. Immediately, I summoned the nurse and was wheeled into the delivery room.

When the nurse asked me if I wanted to call my husband, I shook my head. I didn't want George driving over now, especially since he would have to wake my parents at such a late hour to watch our children. Instead, I prayed that the baby wouldn't arrive until morning. As the hours ticked by, however, I was confronted with the fact that the doctors had given this baby no medical hope; if God didn't perform a miracle, this baby would die like all the others.

Throughout the night—between contractions—I repeated my Scripture verse over and over, allowing His peace to strengthen me and to fill me with hope once again.

A few hours later, as the morning light slowly filtered into the room, I realized I was still in labor. I phoned George, who immediately dropped off our children at my parents' home and rushed to my side. By the time he arrived, I was experiencing excruciating back pain. George stood behind me, locking his arms below mine to help support me during my labor.

Two hours later, one little foot pushed through, then another as I had a breech delivery. A nurse held my baby boy up, and all I could see was a little bluish blob that remained silent: He wasn't breathing. Within seconds, waiting specialists whisked him away.

Unsure of what the outcome would be, I let my head fall back onto my pillow. I was spiritually and physically exhausted. Now all George and I could do was pray.

After I was released from the hospital, George and I made daily three-hour round trips to see our son, whom we named Timothy. He was a four-pound, fair-skinned baby with light eyes and a sprinkling of light hair. During the following week after his birth, Timothy was given 38 blood exchanges, unheard of for such a small baby. Grimly, my doctor explained that with all the different donated blood he received—mostly from college students—they didn't know what impurities Timothy might have picked up. Yet, he was our little cherub, and whenever I saw him, I stroked the side of his head and prayed, continuing to trust and hope in God for a miracle.

Then, when Timothy was ten days old, the doctor phoned us in the middle of the night with the frightening news that Timothy's organs were failing, and he was now on a respirator because he stopped breathing. The doctor only hoped we could make it to the hospital to be with our baby before he died.

All the way there, I squeezed George's hand as hot tears rolled down my cheeks. I thought about Betty Jean and Jonathan. I had had faith that they would live, too, and yet...

"The baby's going to die!" I said, sobbing.

"No," George responded, his voice resolute. Then, after reminding me of God's reassurance at the rally and the prayer of faith I made, he challenged me. "No more tears. We're going to trust God for a miracle."

His resolve strengthened mine. Then, to encourage our faith, George began singing one of our favorite songs, "How Great Is Our God." His deep resonant voice rang out, and I joined him in the familiar words: "How Great is our God, How great is His name, He's the greatest One, Forever the same, He rolled back the waters of the mighty Red Sea, And He said I'll never leave you, Put your trust in Me." After singing it over and over again, the words slowly began to buoy my weary spirit.

We arrived at the hospital and sprang up the steps to the second floor, not bothering to wait for an elevator. Pushing through the door to the prenatal intensive care unit, we hurried to our baby's side.

I flinched. Little Timothy was almost unrecognizable. Lying limply on his back in an incubator, his body was attached to a machine, and a tube ran to his nose. His neck and abdomen were distended, and steel plates were pressed against his lips. Helplessly, we stood beside him as fears stirred and threatened to resurface in me.

I knew that hundreds of Christians were praying for Timothy, yet I wrestled with my faith once again: *Should I have allowed this baby to be born, only to suffer and die? Had I done the right thing?*

Although I felt many different emotions, I knew I would have to choose to trust God through this dark valley. I always said that I trusted God, but I knew that was only true if I didn't have all the answers. Once again, my faith would have to operate in the dark, putting into action the real meaning of trust. For now, all I could understand was that His still, small voice seemed to whisper in my heart, *Just trust me.*

The next day, despite the doctor's predictions, Timothy had rallied and was still alive. Then, three days later, he started breathing on his own and was taken off the respirator. Yet the battle was far from over. The doctor explained that not only had they never had a baby survive with his problems, even if he did, he would probably end up severely retarded due to the lack of blood and oxygen he had suffered. "For all the money you're going to end up spending on this baby," the doctor finally surmised, "you could have bought a house on the French Riviera."

Then he asked if he could pull the plug.

My mouth tightened as I stared back at him wordlessly, stubbornly. Then George shook his head, giving the doctor a resounding "No."

The days turned into weeks and little Timothy continued to hang on. Finally, when he was two months old, the doctor shook his head, apologizing that Timothy was still alive.

Immediately George retorted, "He's going to be a straight-A kid."

The doctor shrugged, then handed me my tiny son. Cradling him in my arms, I returned home with George, refusing to accept the doctor's verdict.

Within a month, however, I noticed a lump bulging out of Timothy's lower groin. I took him to the doctor, who discovered a hernia that required bilateral surgery. Because he weighed only five pounds, he was given a local anesthesia during the two-hour operation. Fortunately, the procedure went smoothly.

Although we determined to love and treat Timothy like a normal infant, he soon began acting far differently from our other children when they were small. Several times a day, he crossed his arms or legs and extended them rigidly straight out, shaking them for 30 to 60 seconds each time.

Feeding Timothy was another problem: He was so small and wasn't able to suck very well; just to get an ounce of milk in him took forever. Fortunately, my other children had a special love and interest in Timothy, doing whatever they could to help. Mary Ann especially became like a second mother to him, rocking and feeding him whenever she had the chance.

I came across a book at the local library that I read to my older children. It was a special encouragement to me during this time. The book was about a little boy who planted some carrot seeds. His older brother and parents discouraged him, telling him the carrots would never grow. Refusing to give up, the boy watered the seeds, believing that one day he would see them sprout. At the end of the story, there was a picture of the boy, filling a large wheelbarrow full of the carrots he had harvested.

Over and over again I read the book to our children to bolster my own faith and to encourage me to trust God for Timothy's total healing.

When Timothy was 4 months old—still unable to hold a bottle or to roll over—one of the hernias returned, requiring surgery again. This time, after the doctor gave him a general anesthesia, we almost lost him.

Shortly afterwards, George decided to return to the Worcester church as pastor again. Since his departure 15 months earlier, things had not gone well at the church, and the new pastor was ready to lock the doors and close it down. Perhaps the young people—many of whom were no longer attending—had felt too strong an allegiance towards us.

We still lived in the summer home which my father now had legally turned over to us. Because it was debt-free, George mortgaged the home, using some of the money to keep the community houses going. Then he invested the rest.

One afternoon, when Timothy was 11 months old, I left him sleeping on the sofa and went outside to mow the grass. A few minutes later, I heard a loud, angry wail. Rushing inside, I discovered Timothy on the floor, unhurt. Breaking into a wide smile, I realized that he had finally rolled over! Scooping him up into my arms, I thanked God for my continuing miracle.

The medical world felt differently. A few weeks later, I took Timothy to see the best pediatrician I could find. The doctor's prognosis wasn't promising. Even though Timothy had started rolling over, and the rigidity in his limbs had disappeared, the doctor thought the slow physical development indicated slow mental development as well.

When Timothy was 2 years old, I began taking a few college courses again. By this time he spoke a few incomprehensible words and was walking, although his legs turned out from his knee joints. Now I was taking Timothy to the cerebral palsy clinic at Children's Hospital in Boston. Two physical therapists in our church taught me exercises I could do with him; gradually, I began seeing some improvement.

Meanwhile, the Jesus Movement was starting to slow down. Although hundreds of people had been saved, and a few had entered the ministry or become missionaries, the going hadn't always been easy. Many were coming off of drugs or were from dysfunctional backgrounds, and they sometimes had a hard time shaking their past demons—two even committed suicide.

It hadn't always been easy for my children, either. Recently, George had taken in an alcoholic to live with us. Later the man told some state troopers that the mafia was coming to kill him. That afternoon I met my children after school, my face tight and serious. Gently I explained that they couldn't go home yet: The house was surrounded by state troopers, hidden in the brush. Eight hours later the alcoholic confessed that he had made up the whole thing. Nevertheless, it was terribly unsettling for all of us, but especially for 8-year-old Mary Ann.

Another time, an enormous woman began visiting our church, finally confessing to me that she was a witch. She explained that she enjoyed our meetings, but her spirits had told her that her mission in life was to kill my husband. A few weeks later, after one of our church services, I was exiting down the steps with Mary Ann and Timothy when the woman stopped me: "I have a knife, and I'm going to kill your husband." An eight-inch knife flashed before me as I clutched my children's hands firmly. Without saying a word, I hastened down the steps.

Although the woman never did manage to harm my husband, it was another unsettling experience for Mary Ann, who was old enough to understand what was happening.

The Jesus Movement lasted about three years, and we rode the wave to the end. Eventually, we closed the coffeehouse and turned it into a church fellowship hall. Brass light fixtures replaced the nautical scenery, and the blue walls were painted a cream color. Meanwhile, many of the young people had gone to college, married, and settled down. Soon our congregation consisted of professionals who were serious, upright citizens. Although I appeared to be a model pastor's wife, it had taken me years of struggle and confession before I finally was able to let go of my resentment of the constant intrusions into my husband's life. I definitely bonded more with the people, but I still had feelings of insecurity at times. These feelings often prevented me from truly having a deep love for the people whom God was calling me to serve.

Meanwhile, our children were growing up, too. George, Jr., now 13, talked his father into buying him a truck. He then hired someone to drive for him, and he and Charlie scoured the city asking people if they could clean their cars or cellars, attics, or garages. He was developing into quite a businessman. Mary Ann, a bright and sensitive 9-year-old, still loved to visit with the elderly and encourage the women in the community houses with little treats whenever she could.

We also were growing older. As the next year flew by, and George's 40th birthday approached, I could see definite signs of fatigue. After pastoring for 15 years and running

Camp Woodhaven in the summers, he had never had a vacation. Finally, he decided to resign as director of the camp, easing the pressure somewhat.

I knew he needed a diversion as well. So, right before his birthday on April 25, I saw an ad in our local Worcester newspaper offering sailing lessons for $25. I signed him up for lessons once a week as a birthday present.

It was just the thing George needed; he took to the sea like a sailor. An avid reader, he also spent most of his free time at the library reading every book he could find on the subject.

When George's ten weeks of sailing lessons were over, he signed up for a course on ocean sailing. Soon my husband was lost in dreams of sailing into the Caribbean, with the tropical breezes blowing at his back.

Meanwhile, I finished my A.A. degree in secretarial studies. But it wasn't typing that God had in store for me next. Instead, He was about to release me into a ministry that would stretch, fulfill, and allow me to be used in a capacity I never thought possible.

Chapter 7

The Vision

On a clear September day I knelt by our gold love seat on the hardwood floor in our bedroom. Soon the refreshing presence of God settled in my midst, easing the restlessness I felt since my college classes had ended. After worshipping for several minutes, I waited quietly before Him.

Out of nowhere an unexpected thought entered my mind. It had to do with Women's Aglow, a nationwide inter-denominational group of Christians who met for encourage-ment and ministry. I had heard wonderful reports about the organization and its members, but I never had the opportu-nity to actually attend one of their meetings. All I knew was that they met once a month and had testimonies, a speaker, and a time of prayer. Strangely, I couldn't shake the growing conviction that I should start a chapter in Worcester.

I pushed the notion aside: I was a behind-the-scenes worker, assisting our church wherever possible as a secre-tary, hostess, pianist, and janitor. I had never been a ministry person before; I didn't even teach Sunday school. Instead, I was by my husband's side in everything he did, comfortable and committed in my support role. Surely God couldn't be calling me into something completely separate from George.

The thought persisted. When I talked with George about it later that day, he encouraged me to look into it. I contacted the Women's Aglow regional director and received the necessary paperwork to get started. Soon I had recruited

12 women from different denominations to become board members, and three pastors to become our advisors.

Three weeks later, after attending a short training session, we had our first meeting in Worcester. Seventy-five women from different denominations attended—some from no church at all. We gathered in the local library and enjoyed pastry and coffee. Several of us gave our testimonies; I shared the story of Timothy, now 3 years old, who had been given no hope of living. I explained that he had been diagnosed with cerebral palsy, and that I was still trusting God for his total healing. I hoped this would encourage them to trust God for what was going on in their lives as well. My staff and I prayed with those who came forward for ministry.

From then on, I held meetings once a month, enjoying this new outlet. Even Mary Ann loved to pitch in, helping with name tags and hospitality. I also loved the strong business structure of Aglow, and I learned many facets of how to run a group successfully. I never had been a leader or even sat in on a board meeting. I was the one who always prepared the coffee and pastry for other board members. Now I was leading one myself, and the women who attended seemed genuinely happy about it. Also, for the first time, I felt free to develop close friendships with these board members, easing the loneliness I sometimes felt as a pastor's wife.

After a challenging year of being president of the local Worcester chapter, I was approved to be the president of Women's Aglow of New England. Besides my local Aglow responsibilities, I was now required to travel to different states, training women who were interested in starting new chapters. So far, there were only five other chapters in New England.

As new chapters began, I was often their first speaker. Surprisingly, people seemed genuinely moved by my message. I shared my trials and victories, and prayed that my words would speak to the unsaved who were there. I remembered my original commitment to share about Jesus with someone every day. I didn't want to stand before God in eternity, realizing I had missed an opportunity to share about Him with someone who was searching. I prayed that I would be God's instrument to impact the lives of as many of the unsaved as possible.

Soon I was thriving in my new challenge, doing all my household responsibilities as fast as possible in order to get back to my Aglow work—planning retreats and leadership training seminars, speaking, forming a solid New England Board, and helping others start new chapters. By the end of my first year as president, there were 13 new chapters throughout New England.

Yet God was doing something much deeper in me than simply developing my leadership and organizational abilities. As I ministered to other women, God began ministering to me. With this came the realization that my own imagination had crippled me for so many years, making me feel unwanted as a child and terribly insecure as a wife. Slowly, as God used me in the lives of others, my own needs began to be met. I discovered that the deeper my security became in Jesus, the more secure I felt as a person. It was another necessary step in order for God's future purposes in my life to be accomplished.

Meanwhile, George continued to pursue his sailing, even making plans to build a sailboat. As he found release in this new outlet and saw the transformation in my life, his own spirits slowly rejuvenated as well.

Still, our own mission call was only a vague memory. While George was enjoying his new diversion, I became more interested in reaching out to other American women than to those across the seas. Even attending an international Aglow conference in Seattle did nothing to spark my interest. At the lovely banquet, a painted clothespin doll was placed beside each place setting, representing different women throughout the world. Fastening my eyes on my doll, I noticed that she was black and wore a red dress. Yet it did nothing to ignite my own mission call. The flame had long since gone out, especially now that I was so caught up in what was happening with Women's Aglow in New England. Eventually, I tucked the doll into my suitcase, not because I was moved by the plight of the world's unsaved Africans, but because I planned to give it to my daughter as a gift.

A few weeks after the conference, on a chilly Saturday morning in October, a chapter in New Hampshire was meeting. I was to be their speaker, and I had been praying for several months for a special anointing on the message I was to share. Now, as I stood in the front of a small hotel room, facing a group of about 60 women, I felt confident—confident that God's anointing would be there, and that His power would speak through me.

I was not prepared for what happened. As I spoke about the love that Mary felt when she washed the feet of Jesus with her hair, my words fell flat. There was no anointing. No power. Nothing. God seemed to have taken off. Although a few people came forward for prayer and several said I did a good job, I felt completely humiliated. I never wanted to speak again.

The next day I was home alone, scrubbing my bathroom floor and thinking about the miserable experience I had in New Hampshire. If God called me to this ministry and I had spent months in advance preparing to speak, where in the world was He when I needed Him?

Soon I was pouring my heart out to God, letting Him know exactly how I felt: "Do you know how humiliating it was for the president of Women's Aglow to speak without an anointing?"

Slowly, my mind reflected over my life. In the past, I was very comfortable working in the background. Trusting

God to help me lead and speak to a group of women effectively was always much more difficult. As much as I
enjoyed these new challenges, I knew that if God no longer
wanted to anoint me, then I had better get out. If He wasn't
calling me, I wasn't about to call myself.

Lifting my face heavenward, I announced, "Lord, if
it's not your will for me to speak anymore, I'll just go back
to the Jeanne I once was—I don't mind being the old
Jeanne."

As I continued my housecleaning and began to vacuum, I slowly surrendered my desires to Him: "However
you want to use me, Lord, is okay with me. I only want to
know Your presence."

Soon the presence of God filled me in a powerful
way. So awesome was it that I finally shut my vacuum
cleaner off and sank to my knees. Although I had just surrendered my desires to ever speak again, I now felt an overwhelming, compelling desire to preach. An inner boldness
and authority filled my entire being, and I thought about
how much I would have loved to have had this experience
yesterday when I had spoken.

What happened next still amazes me. As I worshipped
God, I suddenly found myself staring at a panoramic picture, like a 360-degree Disneyland screen. I was surrounded
by the vision. My mouth dropped open as dark-faced
women from India encircled me, wearing different-colored
sarees. Their faces were etched in pain and their brown and
hollow eyes filled with longing. It was as though they were
waiting for someone to tell them about Jesus and His love
for them.

A supernatural love for these women engulfed me,
even though I had never met them. So overwhelming was
this love that I knew that I had never—could ever, would
ever—experience any greater love than this for anyone, even
my family. It was so powerful that I felt like a firecracker

ready to explode; it was almost too great for my natural body to contain.

Time seemed to stand still as I sat there trembling and staring out at the sea of faces around me. I wasn't even aware of how many seconds or minutes the vision lasted. I only knew that I was to go to these women and tell them about Jesus.

Raising my hands in worship, tears trickled down my cheeks as I felt humbled by all that I had seen.

Thirty minutes later, I resumed my vacuuming as God's presence slowly dissipated. As I thought about what had transpired, I decided not to tell anyone except my husband. I always was taught to question people who said they had a vision, feeling their experience sounded a little extreme. Besides, how could I explain to others that I had experienced a vision telling me to preach in India when I couldn't even give an anointed message one hour away from where I lived? Not only that, but I had four children, no money and had never even been to a Third World country.

Despite my objections and the fact that my call to missions had been buried for years, I knew I was to go. Perhaps my unanointed message the day before had been a test to see how I would respond; perhaps Satan simply wanted to discourage me. I didn't know the answer. I only knew that if this vision was from God, it would come to pass. For now, everything in me yearned to tell these Indian women about my Lord and Savior.

That evening, as soon as I spotted George coming through the door, I ventured, "Can I go to India?" Without a moment's hesitation he said, "Yes." It was as though I had just asked him to take the garbage out: He didn't appear surprised at all.

My story tumbled out as I told George all that had transpired. His eyes radiated an inner confidence in what I had shared. However, realizing I would feel more secure and better received in India's culture with my husband there, I asked him to accompany me.

George's eyes locked onto mine. "No," he said decidedly. "I'll send you with my blessing, but I don't think it's God's will for me to go."

I nodded in acceptance, acutely aware that we still didn't even have the money to fly me there. We lived on a very low salary and had only $83 in savings, not nearly enough for a round-trip ticket to India. Both of us realized that if God was really in this, He would have to do a miracle.

Still, I knew I needed to do the possible. I phoned my mother, hoping to get in contact with an Indian man who was going to Massachusetts Institute of Technology and who attended her church. I hoped he could tell me if my desire to go to India was a real possibility or not, or give me some contacts if I did go.

Mom wasn't home, yet I didn't want to waste any time. I called my sister Elizabeth, who lived around the corner from her and was always kept abreast of my mother's whereabouts.

Elizabeth was a housewife with three children. Throughout the years, we gradually drifted apart, seeing each other only during holidays. Although I knew she had become quite active in her own local Women's Aglow chapter near Boston and really loved the Lord, I decided not to speak of my plans.

As soon as I heard my sister's voice, I blurted: "Elizabeth, will you go to India with me?"

Why did I say that? I asked myself, completely baffled. But my sister's reaction was even more of a surprise.

"Just this morning," she responded, "I was praying for India...I'll go with you."

A few minutes later, I placed the receiver back in the cradle, biting my lower lip, wondering if I had done the right thing. I was happy to have someone to go with me, yet I wasn't sure how well we would work together. Elizabeth and I weren't exactly two peas in a pod. She was the firstborn—wanted and adored; I was the second—a surprise pregnancy. Growing up, I stood in her shadow as boys waited in line to date her. She was now fashionable and well off. I was poor and wore plain clothes. Nevertheless, I pushed my fears aside, and realized the trip wasn't going to take place anyway unless I received the necessary finances.

The next day, my mother called. Recently, the Department of Environmental Protection had passed new controls affecting my father's electro-plating business. Therefore, he had wanted to sell it and retire early. Now, she explained, he had found a buyer. As a result, he was giving each of his children $1,000.

My heart did a somersault. I had received my airfare!

Soon everything else came together, like dominoes falling into place. After I got a hold of Alex Harris, the Indian man who attended my mother's church, he contacted his mother, a Christian doctor who resided in India. Soon Dr. Harris was able to arrange an itinerary for us, booking us for speaking engagements in churches and retreats. She also invited us to live in her home during our three-week stay.

Before Elizabeth and I left, I prayed for India every chance I could. Unfortunately, by the time we were due to leave, I developed a painful infection in my left ear that I couldn't seem to shake. Therefore, when we finally boarded our plane in January—just over two months since I had experienced my vision—my ear was plugged up with cotton, and I was on medication.

I gazed at Elizabeth sitting in the airplane seat beside me. Her striking brown eyes, a soft touch of make-up, and her thick, long, chestnut hair framed a pretty but tense face. I knew she anticipated this trip, but she also expressed her worry and uncertainty of being in a Third World country.

A few minutes later, as the nose of the plane pointed upward and I felt the powerful thrust of the engines carry us into the sky, nothing could dampen my own spirits—not even the pain in my left ear. I was too caught up in fulfilling the mandate of the vision I had seen. Instead, I was already in India, sharing the love of Jesus with all those eager, hungry faces.

Chapter 8

Fanning the Flame for Missions

Elizabeth and I stepped off the plane in Madras and were greeted by Indians swarming around us like bees, hoping to carry our luggage. Fortunately, we were soon rescued by Dr. Harris. A plump, middle-aged woman with black hair that had a touch of white, she was warm and outgoing. And we soon discovered that she possessed a deep spiritual sensitivity.

After we located our luggage, Dr. Harris motioned for one of the young men to help us, and then escorted us safely outside. Stepping into the bright sunshine, I was barraged by a variety of sights and sounds. In the distance I could hear the sound of high-pitched music, and I could smell the rubbish burning and the outdoor cooking. Cows roamed freely through narrow streets clogged with cars. But it was the women who really caught my attention. As they scurried along the busy sidewalks in their colorful sarees, I studied them intently. These were the ones I was called to know. This was why I had come.

Once we arrived at Dr. Harris' home, Elizabeth and I were pleasantly surprised. The doctor had just put in indoor plumbing and running water—real luxuries in India. Yet, we soon realized we had a few other things to become accustomed to. Besides the lizards that were sometimes found crawling in our bathroom, there was a lot of thievery. As a result, bars covered our windows. But because there were no screens or glass on any of them, nothing could be left in sight; otherwise someone might be tempted to put a stick between the bars, trying to steal what they saw.

During the night, Dr. Harris locked our belongings in a separate room on the second floor of her home. Then, as we huddled in bed under our mosquito net, a watchman walked the streets with an iron cane, trying to discourage any thieves from visiting the neighborhood. Throughout the night we could hear him pass by our window: *thump, thump, thump.*

Meanwhile, Elizabeth was plagued with terrible fear, even wrapping her face in a towel when she went to bed so that she couldn't see anything. During the first night we were there, she threw her arms around me, wondering if we would ever get home to see our husbands and children again.

The next day, Dr. Harris gave us several colorful sarees to wear whenever we went outside. To wear this traditional Indian attire, however, we first had to put on a tight-fitting under-blouse, then wrap ourselves in rolls and rolls of material. It felt a bit suffocating, so I was grateful we were in the midst of India's coolest season.

Elizabeth and I followed our itinerary, and God gave us many opportunities to minister to the precious Indian women. During the day, because of the painful infection in my ear, I tried to rest as much as possible, allowing plenty of time to pray about each evening's message. Often I spoke on God's unfailing love for these women, and how they could put their hope and faith in Him.

As the days flew by, however, it was Elizabeth who continued to amaze me. Despite the fact that she still battled fears of being in a Third World country, God was using her powerfully. Just before I spoke, she always gave a testimony. Although I never told her in advance what I would share, she always confirmed my message through what she said. Elizabeth spent hours weeping and praying for the women who flocked forward for ministry.

I couldn't believe it: Here I was, praying all day while my sister socialized with every Indian who set foot on our doorstep seeking fellowship. Yet, she was impacting so many of their lives. Elizabeth had never done anything like this before, but she was full of boundless energy and compassion, blossoming into a real woman of God, confirming to both of us that she was called to be in India during this time.

One weekend, we gave a two-day conference sponsored by the Full Gospel Women of India. More than 800 women dressed in colorful sarees attended, open and hungry for the things of God, just like the women in my vision. During lunch time, as we feasted on a rice dish seasoned with nuts, vegetables, and spices wrapped in banana leaves, my heart overflowed with love for these women. Never before had I experienced anything like it.

Dr. Harris tried to avoid letting us see the poorer class of India, but she couldn't protect us completely. Once when I was in downtown Madras, a year-old baby sat covered with dirt and flies on the edge of a sidewalk. What surprised me, though, was how people stepped right over her, not missing a beat or even "seeing" the child. I also observed children across the street from where we lived, rummaging through garbage from a wedding, opening banana leaves and separating the scraps of food. Dr. Harris was very embarrassed when she realized what I observed, yet it made me further aware of the tremendous needs in India—not just spiritually but physically as well.

Elizabeth and I flew home three weeks later. We had come to India as sisters. We returned to the United States as soul mates for life, changed forever by what had taken place in the 17 places we had spoken.

Now that we were home and reunited with our families again, I assumed that chapter in my life was over, and that things would return to normal. Instead, something was born in me that wouldn't go away. For my own mission call—pushed down for so many years—was now stirring and rising to the surface, longing to break through.

Everywhere I looked now, I saw a mission field. With it came the realization that God was giving me the same capacity of love for the people of Worcester as I had for the Indian women. Unlike my previous evangelism efforts, it was a different capacity of love than I had ever experienced. For the first time, I saw people through God's eyes and through His unconditional love for them. Even my own congregation—toward whom I had always lacked a deep love and bond—was now seen in a new light, as God's chosen and precious individuals.

I noticed another change in me as well. The need in India had so impressed me that I discovered I lost my taste for material possessions. As an American woman, it seemed as though I never had enough; now I wanted to rid myself of anything that cluttered my life and took time from serving God.

Meanwhile, Elizabeth was experiencing changes of her own. Soon after we returned home, she became more involved with Women's Aglow, speaking and leading Bible studies. Eventually, she attended Bible school and later was given an honorary degree.

I also spoke at Women's Aglow meetings and in my church, sharing my enthusiasm about my missionary experience to India. We started taking up a missions offering each month.

After I had been home a few weeks, I told a long-time minister friend of ours how excited I was about missions.

"Why are you doing this mission thing?" he asked with an edge to his voice. "Trying to compete with your husband in the ministry?"

Startled, I gave him a long look. All my married life, this minister had known me as the wife who stood in the background, supporting my husband in whatever he did. Yet I knew God was now requiring more of me.

"No," I finally responded, my voice sounding resolute. "Besides, we're always on a mission field. It's wherever we are and wherever we go." For as much as I wanted to, I knew I wasn't returning to India tomorrow. Despite the fact that George had felt called to be a missionary at the time of his conversion, nothing was stirring in him yet. And so, whoever was in my pathway now became my "India." That was my mission.

Still, I felt that I needed to prepare for the mission field by getting further education. To do this, I realized I had to give up something I deeply loved: the Women's Aglow presidency of New England. I loved the people, the beautiful luncheons, conferences, and all the encouragement I received personally, but I knew I was no longer content. Although I decided to continue in my less demanding role as local president in Worcester, I knew God was leading me in a different direction. Little did I realize just how much Women's Aglow had already taught and prepared me for the women's ministry God had planned for me in the future.

Soon a friend and I visited a seminary an hour and a half from home. Since my friend had an interview there, I decided to speak with the Missions Director about enrolling in the school's Missions program.

After telling the director I was a pastor's wife with four children, and a tremendous burden for missions, he asked me my children's ages. After I told him that they were now 16, 14, 12 and 5, his face became tight and serious. "Your mission field is your home and children. Go home and take care of them."

Disappointment now clouded my vision. Not only was my husband disinterested in becoming a missionary, now a Missions Director had informed me that I shouldn't be in school. *Was the hope of being used by God on the mission field just my own imagination?* I wondered.

Even George recognized that God was moving through our church, using missions as a catalyst. The more money we gave in that area, the more the general budget began to mushroom. Soon we were no longer struggling financially either as a family or as a church. Already, through generous offerings, we were building a church in India and sending three boys through Bible school there. Still, we had excess funds that we didn't know what to do with.

It wasn't long before George was thinking seriously of taking his own mission trip. While reading about sailing in the Carribean, he came across information on Haiti. Since it was only 700 miles off the coast of Miami, he felt it might be an easy place to begin. Often he wondered how Haiti would compare with my missionary experience in India.

Two months after I returned home from India, George decided to fly to Haiti with one of our deacons. While they were gone, questions swirled through my mind. Haiti, I knew, was considered part of South America, where George had once felt called to be a missionary. What if he fell in love with the Haitian people? What if we ended up going there as missionaries someday? As thrilled as I knew I would feel to be on the mission field again, it made me wonder: *Would I be able to transfer my love for the Indian people to the people of Haiti?*

When George returned from Haiti a week later, he seemed deeply moved by the plight of the people, overwhelmed by their need. Yet there were no foreseeable plans for us to become missionaries. Although George was willing to step out and obey God at any cost, he wasn't sure yet what our involvement should be.

Meanwhile, I continued to suffer from the same ear infection I had before I left for India. My ear drum had swollen to seven times its size and the infection had reached close to my brain. Finally, I had surgery performed in which a doctor fashioned a new ear drum and did a skin graft. The doctor didn't think I would ever hear out of that ear again; fortunately, he proved to be wrong.

That summer we went on our first family vacation in our new sailboat, the "Mia Carita"—meaning "My Love" in Italian. It was hard to believe that five years earlier we were penniless paupers, not even owning a house. Now we felt like middle-class Americans.

Although it was wonderful to have our family together, I was seasick before I even set foot on our sailboat. Just standing on the shore looking at the waves made me nauseated. So while George and the children enjoyed the ocean view, I remained down in our cabin praying for missions, too sick to do anything else.

Missions continued to be my all-consuming passion. Eventually I decided to take my own trip to Haiti, looking for ways George and I could get involved. The three-and-a-half-hour flight from New York to Port-au-Prince was a real experience. The plane was jammed with bourgeois Haitians decked in silk suits and gold jewelry, and struggling with stereos, televisions, and expensive luggage. Soon I would discover how enormous the gulf is between the rich and poor in Haiti.

When I landed in Port-au-Prince, the conditions were equally overwhelming. The city was filled with stench, burning rubble, and choking diesel fumes. People urinated freely in the streets. Hot water and electricity were considered rare luxuries.

After I gathered my luggage, I went outside and was followed by two children rubbing their bellies with one hand and stretching out the other: "I am hungry, blanc. Give me a dollar." Shortly I would discover that children who experienced "Vant plen"—eating enough to feel full—were a rare occurrence in this country.

When I returned and shared my experiences regarding the suffering and poverty I had seen, our church began sponsoring several Haitian children and giving money to schools and churches in Haiti. Soon I was busy arranging for small groups from our church to take trips to Haiti as well as overseeing several projects we were helping with there. That provided me with some satisfaction, but I longed for the day when George and I could be on the mission field ourselves. Since I knew we weren't going to the mission field any time soon, I decided the next best thing would be to sell our lovely home and move into the first floor of our church. That way, we would be right on the front lines of ministry, living in the midst of the people we wanted to serve.

When I asked George if he would be willing to move, I pointed out it would be far more convenient for us. And I would be right there, able to work alongside him whenever he needed me. George raised an eyebrow, amazed at the transformation that had taken place in my life. Then he smiled broadly, nodding in agreement.

Nine months after I returned from India, we sold our home. The autumn leaves swirled at our feet as my family and I moved into the church. Immediately I set to work, trying to make it as homey as possible. Off of the hall foyer was an office, kitchen, and large meeting area, which I turned into a living room, filling it with my gold velvet Victorian furniture and an Oriental rug. Off of the living room was a bathroom and several smaller rooms which became our bedrooms.

Because we lived on the main highway of the city, we could often hear police cars and sirens. But I didn't care; I was ecstatic to be in our new "home." People dropped in constantly, needing counseling or hanging around after church to see what was for lunch. I looked upon it as a learning experience; since I never went to Bible school, I considered this to be my missionary training ground.

Meanwhile, my children were plunged into their own mission field, finding themselves in a multi-ethnic neighborhood and part of a minority at their inner-city schools. On the whole—despite a few scrapes and shoves—they adjusted well without complaining. I was particularly pleased that Mary Ann's junior high school teacher attended Women's Aglow and was especially kind to my daughter.

My youngest, 5-year-old Timothy, was also in school. Although he was walking and talking, he still wasn't walking normally and his words were difficult to understand. Nevertheless, he was slowly making progress.

Our new home had a little hallway with two closets— one for George and one for me. Since I only allowed myself to own four outfits in an attempt to simplify my life, I used the rest of the space for missions. Inside, I hung up flags of different countries and pasted magazine articles on the wall which told about elections, famines, or other things I wanted to pray about. Since the closet was just big enough for me to sit in, I shut myself inside every morning for one hour and prayed for missions.

Because I was also sharing about India and Haiti during various speaking engagements, the mission giving began to grow. George felt this money should be funneled through his umbrella organization, George DeTellis Evangelistic Association, rather than the church. I formed a board of two pastors and two businessmen and called ourselves New England and World Missions (N.E.W.), putting into practice the accountability and structure I learned at Women's Aglow.

A few months later, despite the discouragement I received by the Missions Director when I visited the seminary, I decided to return to college. Since there were no mission schools nearby, I decided to go the secular route and major in foreign affairs. This would allow me to study international economics and politics. I knew if I didn't understand what controlled the needs of the people I might eventually work with, I would be ineffective. So I enrolled in three classes at Assumption College, which was only two miles from the church where we lived. Unfortunately, because of my schooling commitment, I had to resign from Women's Aglow altogether.

While George was happy I was continuing my education, I soon discovered that I hated studying politics. At the same time, my international economics class was a big eye opener for me. The more I researched, the more I discovered how the poorest of the poor often are exploited for cheap labor. And because many parts of the world require lots of slaves for heavy labor or to work as domestic servants in their homes, they also want them to remain illiterate.

Although I felt God had called me back to school, I continued to dislike the course material. Every morning as I walked across the college campus, I proclaimed, "God, I love you, and I'll be true to the call of missions in my life. I'll stick it out." Therefore, some nights, after my husband and children went to bed, I put on a pot of coffee and stayed up all night studying. With all of my other responsibilities, I knew it was the only way I could get through college.

Winter, spring, and summer flew by. As George and I remained in a state of perpetual motion, we had little time to observe the effects that living in our church was having on our children. Sometimes when people left, they forgot to lock the front door, allowing drunks or other young people coming off of drugs to wander in during the night. Another time I took in a 20-year-old mentally-disturbed woman, letting her share a bunk bed with Mary Ann. All of this, including one alcoholic who lived with us for a month, became quite upsetting for my daughter.

Years later, I realized it shouldn't have been necessary for Mary Ann to put up with all the "strays" we had coming in and out of our home. At the time, however, George and I were both naive and overzealous, unaware of the effects that this must have been having on our children. Many times we were too busy trying to take care of other people that our children were lost in the shuffle. And because I felt I had to be in church every Sunday night as well as midweek meetings, my children ended up getting to bed terribly late, and were exhausted for school the following morning.

Our church congregation knew we had three children but were unaware we had four. We required our children to be in church each Sunday, but Charlie would slip into the last row just before the service started, then lay his head back and go to sleep. Then, just before the final invitation, he would sneak out. Soon Charlie began hanging out with a bad crowd, dabbling in alcohol.

One day we received a call from Charlie's high school: Our son hadn't been in school for 50 days. Since we had observed him leaving for school every morning with his books, George and I were completely shocked. It was the first time we were aware that something was seriously wrong. Fortunately, after a strong "talking to" by his father, Charlie attended school faithfully. Meanwhile, every morning after he left, I made his bed for him, placing my hands on the sheets each time, hoping my love and prayers would change his life. By the end of the year, even though Charlie still hadn't surrendered his life to the Lord, he did manage to pass the tenth grade.

My greatest encouragement was little Timothy, whose speech and coordination continued to improve. George, Jr., was also doing well and had adjusted easily to our move. Still I wondered if all the sacrifice was worth it. Here I was, married with four children, tired all the time from pulling all-nighters and trying to go to school. Yet George didn't feel the same deep desire to become a missionary as I did. And now, after moving into the church, feeling it would be good preparation for missionary service, Charlie had gotten himself involved with the wrong group of kids. On top of that, Mary Ann was finding some of her experiences living in the inner-city unsettling.

Nevertheless, my dream of someday being a missionary persisted. Deep down, I knew that God was calling me to the mission field as certainly as I knew He had saved me.

I just had no idea how it was going to happen.

Chapter 9

Taking the Next Step

George sat hunched over his desk, a quiet pain in his eyes. He had returned from yet another trip to Haiti—one of several he had taken over the past three years. We weren't on the mission field yet, but George's interest in Haiti had continued to escalate. Our church was sponsoring children there, helping to feed and educate them. Yet each time George visited them, he returned discouraged. After observing the children's bloated bellies and runny noses, he felt they weren't receiving adequate care.

I could see his frustration mounting. Locking his eyes on mine, he finally declared: "If anything is ever going to get done in Haiti, we're going to have to do it ourselves."

Surprise registered on my face, and a new surge of hope rose within me. Yet things were finally going so well at home that I couldn't imagine George wanting to leave. Our former hippies from the Jesus Movement had blossomed into a mature group of professional middle- and upper-class individuals. The church budget had grown along with them, allowing George to receive a good salary with every imaginable benefit. For the first time in our married life, we were no longer struggling financially. I knew George was concerned about the plight of the Haitian children, but I also knew it was a lot easier to do what we were already doing: writing checks to support other ministries.

And I had finally graduated from Assumption College with a degree in Foreign Affairs. At my graduation, the president of the school presented me with a dozen roses. He heard I was a pastor's wife with four children and was going to school because I believed I had a call to missions.

My professors encouraged me to begin work on a graduate degree at nearby Clark University, majoring in International Development. How grateful I was for their encouragement. I still had memories of my eighth-grade home room teacher who told me I wasn't college material. Despite her gloomy predictions, God had enabled me to excel in college so I could better prepare myself for His future plans for me. Several weeks later, I was even more elated when I was not only accepted at Clark University, but was given a scholarship to cover my tuition.

Meanwhile, our children were all doing well. George, Jr. was attending a local college, majoring in business, while Mary Ann was diligently taking college classes during high school in order to graduate early. And now, not only was 8-year-old Timothy doing well in school, but his speech and coordination were almost completely normal. Little did I realize how much I needed the miracle of his life in the years ahead to encourage others who were without hope.

Charlie had also turned his life around after he consented to let my mother pray for him at a summer camp meeting. Moved by her love and concern, he decided to give his life to Jesus for one week, on a trial basis. By the end of the week, his whole outlook on life had changed so dramatically that he eventually moved up to the front row of our church.

The summer before I started school at Clark University, I took over as president of Camp Woodhaven. Even though I felt called to missions, I knew I wasn't going anywhere yet.

Although the summer camp had been operating since 1947, there had never been a chapel. My dream was to build one. After praying for God's direction, I formed a picture of the chapel in my mind: It was made of natural wood and was situated on the highest point of the land. Because of the cold New England winters, it had lots of large glass windows to let in the sunlight, as well as to view the breathtaking countryside. There would also be two sets of sliding glass doors on each side of the chapel so an extension could eventually be built for a year-round retreat house. It would have an office and bathroom facilities. My goal was to see the chapel built by the following summer. To encourage myself, I kept remembering the story of the little boy and the carrot seeds.

Meanwhile, after three years of living in our church, we were encouraged to move out since the space was now needed for an office and Sunday school rooms. But since we had sold our home, housing prices had escalated so much that we couldn't find anything under $100,000.

One afternoon I looked at ten houses near our church, hoping to find something close so we wouldn't need a second vehicle. But everything was too expensive. Discouraged, I turned around in the driveway of a large Victorian house, just a mile from our church. An elderly man was raking the lawn.

Popping my head out the car window, I inquired, "Do you know if there are any houses for sale in this neighborhood?"

The old man looked up and nodded. "This house is for sale for $39,500. I won't take a penny less."

Smiling buoyantly, I said I would be back.

The next day George came with me, and we looked inside. The ceilings needed to be redone and the kitchen would have to be renovated, but the house itself was well-built. Immediately, we made arrangements to buy it and move in.

That fall, in the midst of settling into our 10-room, Victorian home, and working with an architect on building plans for the chapel, I started graduate school at Clark University. Challenged by my new course material, I learned how governments develop as well as the social, economic, and cultural changes that can occur. Even though I was getting my information from a secular viewpoint, I tried to adapt what I was learning to my missionary calling.

Meanwhile, George took another trip to Haiti, this time looking at five acres of land that were for sale. Frustrated over the conditions he saw, he was becoming more serious about starting his own mission, staffing it with volunteers.

Encouraged by George's mounting interest, I decided to research Haiti myself. Soon I was caught up in its dramatic history.

Once known as the Pearl of the Antilles, the country had been ruled by the Spanish since 1492, when Columbus first set foot on the land. After forcing the native Indians into slavery—who eventually died through slaughter and disease—the Spanish imported Africans and made them slaves instead. As a result, large amounts of coffee, sugar, and mahogany were exported, producing even more wealth for Spain.

Finally, in 1697, Spain lost a war to France and ceded one third of the country to them, which the French named Haiti. The other two thirds is known today as the Dominican Republic.

In 1804, the leaders of the revolt against France invited the voodoo priests to come among them to perform a voodoo ceremony that would dedicate Haiti and the generations to come to practice voodoo. Haiti became the first black republic in the world. They feared that France would return and eventually overtake them again. J. J. Dessalines, the head of the army, commanded his men to kill every white man and burn every home. Therefore, every Frenchman—including doctors, teachers, and landowners— were destroyed, along with every plantation and irrigation system. (At the time, 95 percent of the land was being irri- gated.)

Unfortunately, the black Haitians had destroyed the very people who could have educated and assisted them in organizing their own government. Now all the machinery that could have been effective in helping them become a nation was gone. Instead, with their last bit of resources, they enslaved their own people and forced them to build a fortress called the Citadel, to protect themselves from Napoleon.

Because other countries still had slavery at this time, they refused to trade with Haiti, for fear of rewarding the slaves' rebellion. Eventually, the only way this new black republic could ever negotiate trade relations with anyone was to repay France the enormous sum of 60 million francs for the loss of life and property.

Still, after Haiti's initial independence, things went well at first. With only 500,000 people, every black African was given his own piece of land. Food was plentiful, and the soil was rich and productive. Soon, however, the nation became quickly overpopulated because every man had at least three wives to produce children for labor.

Today, 7.3 million people live in Haiti, and each par- cel of land has been reduced to nearly postage-stamp-size, with only 5 percent of the land under irrigation. A tremen- dous number of trees have been cut down for fuel, causing soil erosion in the mountains, which cover two-thirds of the country.

Now, not only is there a crisis in overpopulation, but most people are unemployed while a few rich families enjoy monopolies on cars, cement, flour, etc. The main tax in the country is on imported goods—there is no annual property tax. And because Haiti has so little to offer the rest of the world, 90 percent of the money from their exports—mainly coffee and mangos—is used to import items for the rich, rather than to build schools or help the poor.

As I researched further, I learned that Haiti has an extractive form of government, taking from the people to enrich itself. Only 50 percent of the children attended school—25 percent of those in private schools. Each year the population increased by 500,000, although no new schools were being built. This meant fewer and fewer children had the opportunity to learn and were therefore more easily subject to exploitation.

Sickness and disease also abounded because of the shortage of medical professionals. I was surprised to read that there are more Haitian doctors in Canada than in all of Haiti. If a doctor remained in Haiti, he usually made no more than a person working at a fast-food restaurant. The number one killer in the country was diarrhea, followed by malaria, tuberculosis, typhoid fever, and other tropical diseases. Yet, whenever the rich needed medical help, they simply flew to Miami.

Jean Claude Duvalier—also known as Baby Doc—was the present dictator, and I was told that tremendous corruption surrounded him. Nevertheless, I was aware that nothing was hopeless with God, especially since it seemed like a miracle that the Haitian people were surviving at all.

After a busy year at college, I was able to dedicate The Chapel at Camp Woodhaven the following summer on August 31. It was exactly as I pictured it in my mind one year ago. Brass chandeliers and wall sconce lighting added to its beauty. I also bought orange chairs in order to remind me of the story about the little boy and the carrot seeds.

At the dedication, I encouraged everyone to plant and water their seeds. One day, the harvest would come and then, they too, would see their carrots. The event was especially meaningful to me because my beloved grandmother attended. It was to be one of the last special times we had together since she suffered a fatal stroke the next month.

Meanwhile, I continued with my education and completed my second year of graduate work. Then, in November, George and I both flew to Haiti with a group of 24, including members from our church and Haitians from the First Baptist Church. Laden with gifts, we visited several works we were supporting.

For three years, George had kept his eye on the same five acres of land that was still for sale. Just before we were due to leave, we viewed it again. That evening our group gathered at a restaurant in Port-au-Prince. Placing my hand on George's, I ventured, "Honey, what are we going to do about the land?"

George looked at me and smiled. "When I walked on the land today, I felt God tell me, 'George, go with it.'"

My heart leapt inside. For five years, ever since returning from India, I dreamt of the day when George and I could serve God together on the mission field. George went on to explain that we would only live in Haiti for three months to get the work started, but it was a stepping stone to what I prayed would become permanent.

The next few months were a flurry of activity as we tried to raise $7,500 for the land. In the meantime, we were able to come up with $1,000 to buy a 1970 truck, which we planned on shipping to Haiti.

We purchased the land on St. Patrick's Day, March 17, 1982, four months after making the decision. George took photographs of all the children in the surrounding villages near our new property—villages that were without schools, churches, or clinics. After getting the children's names and most of their birth dates (some had been lost through fires and floods), he assigned each of them a number, hoping to persuade individuals to eventually sponsor them.

Soon we were faced with the realities of what we were attempting. We had little money, no missionaries, no experience in building anything except a chapel, and we were just informed that our truck was not yet approved by Haitian customs because it was more than five years old.

At the same time, I reminded myself that a few years ago my dream of working alongside George as a missionary seemed almost impossible.

Now we were close to making that dream a reality.

Chapter 10

Hope in God

George stared at the photograph of an 8-year-old Haitian girl and sighed deeply. Her name was Manise—child number 1. Looking over his shoulder, I noticed that she had all the signs of malnutrition: red hair, a bloated belly, and dry cracked skin. I also knew that Manise had an absentee father who had deserted her mother.

George had sent Manise's picture to a woman who requested information about sponsoring a child. In the letter he enclosed, he told her it would cost $15 a month to provide the child with food, clinic care, books, and a uniform. Today George had received her response, saying that $15 was too much for her to commit. Along with the letter, she returned the picture of Manise.

George stared into space, and I could feel his frustration. Recently, he was shaken when a close ministry friend of ours had scoffed at our decision to start a mission, wondering how we would raise the necessary finances required to keep it going. Yet, after much prayer, God gave George the reassurance that if we kept our hearts right with Him, He would give us what we needed for the mission.

It was the same counsel I received just days earlier from a wise and able businessman. He also explained that if I kept my heart right with God, I would never have to worry about His provision.

From then on, I decided to spend more time in right relationship with God than in counting the envelopes of money that might come in each day. As a result, I chose to only look at the finances once a month, praying and trusting God. At the same time, George and I also felt the weight of responsibility on our shoulders. We realized that the blessing on the Haitian people would be contingent on our relationship with God.

Now, as George eyed Manise's picture, he pointed his index finger at her and announced, "We're going to sponsor that child."

I smiled broadly, feeling the tension fade away. However, I knew this was only one child out of hundreds who still needed to be sponsored. Nevertheless, it was a beginning.

Soon we had a missions convention in our church to raise financial support and recruit a few volunteers to work with us in Haiti. Two couples in their mid-20s agreed to come for one year—Curt and Cindy Smith, and John and Diane Vrooman. Curt would help direct the work while John would be an asset with his carpentry skills. Both women were registered nurses. How grateful we were to have them join us.

After the convention, we were surprised when our son, Charlie, now 19 years old, asked my husband if he could come to Haiti, too. George agreed, and I looked forward to having both Timothy and Charlie with us. George, Jr., who was now a junior at Florida International University, and Mary Ann, who was attending a local community college, would remain behind.

Although I had completed my course work for my master's degree, I still needed to work on my thesis. Haiti was the ideal place to do my research, since I planned to write about the role of rural Haitian children in a household economy. I wanted to know exactly how much work—if anything—the children did to contribute to the families' survival. Once I arrived, I hoped to observe the children in action.

Meanwhile, our missionary team met once a week to learn the Creole language. George wrote up a constitution to give to the government of Haiti so that we could be officially recognized. This was advisable because eventually we hoped to build a school, church, and clinic.

Although donations had previously been funneled through our organization named New England and World Missions (N.E.W. Missions), we decided to rename ourselves NEW Missions because God had given us many friends from outside New England to support our new venture.

Just before Christmas—three weeks before our team was scheduled to leave for Haiti—I planned a big lasagna dinner for some pastors and their wives as a way of thanking them for contributing to our mission. As I bustled about the kitchen that morning, Mary Ann appeared, holding her stomach.

"Mom," she groaned, "I don't feel well. I'm in pain."

I brushed her concern aside, certain she was just reacting from the stress of studying for her college finals and our eventual departure. "Maybe you should lie down for a while," I said.

"I really think I need to go to a doctor..."

"You're probably just exhausted from—"

"—No, it's not that."

"Honey, you'll be okay...I've got to keep working now."

Mary Ann's face grew serious. "If you don't take me to the doctor, then I'll get someone else." Then she turned and left.

I let out a long sigh, hoping her sickness would pass. I knew I didn't have the luxury of worrying about her now. Instead, my mind raced over all the evening preparations: My guests were coming from all over New England, and I wanted everything to be perfect.

The hours passed quickly. Then, that afternoon, the phone interrupted my nonstop action. It was a doctor, calling from a nearby clinic. "Your daughter needs emergency surgery," he explained. "She has bilateral cysts on her ovaries that are ready to burst."

Feelings of guilt washed over me as I swallowed hard, trying to absorb the distressing news. I was painfully aware that had Mary Ann listened to me and remained home, her condition could have been far more critical.

How I longed to rush to my daughter's side and be with her. Yet, in two short hours, 40 people were arriving, many of whom were already on their way. How could I cancel on such short notice?

Instead, I called one of Mary Ann's close friends to be with her while I stayed home, putting together the last remaining layers of lasagna.

That evening our guests arrived from all over New England. As I served and mingled with the crowd, I found it hard to concentrate: Here I was, eating a big fancy meal with my friends while my daughter, just a week shy of her 17th birthday, was lying in some hospital bed undergoing surgery.

As my heart hurt for my only daughter, unsettling events from her past raced and repeated in my mind: the day I told her she couldn't go home after school because it was surrounded by state troopers. The times she discovered drunks or drug addicts in our hallway. The weeks she roomed with a mentally-disturbed woman. The alcoholic who had lived with us. Over and over, pangs of guilt plagued me as I remembered how much Mary Ann had never liked the abnormality of our ministry—especially when we lived in the church. And now when she needed me the most, I had let her down.

Shortly after dinner, we received word from the hospital that Mary Ann's surgery had been successful. After our last guest finally departed around 10:30 P.M., George and I jumped in our car and drove through a blinding snowstorm to the hospital.

When we finally entered Mary Ann's room, she appeared groggy. Nevertheless, I detected a quiet pain in her deep brown eyes. Brushing her light brown tousled hair away from her eyes, I looked down upon the sad and pale face of my only daughter.

By the end of the week Mary Ann was released from the hospital and feeling better. George and I moved her into the community house where she wouldn't have to live alone during our stay in Haiti. But a growing concern gnawed at me: If Mary Ann never liked the abnormality of our ministry, how would she fare in a community house with a bunch of women, many from dysfunctional backgrounds?

Yet, I was so certain God was calling us to Haiti that I knew I would have to trust Him to take care of my daughter. However, it was hard to let go. Not only was Mary Ann still recovering from surgery and about to face the pain of her parents' absence, but she was having to make the adjustment to a new environment as well.

On January 6, I hugged my daughter in a tearful good-bye as our small missionary team boarded a plane for Haiti via New York. Inside our luggage, along with a minimum amount of clothing, were five tents, blankets, medical supplies, cooking utensils, a kerosene stove, and a large banner. It also contained several women's uniforms consisting of a light blue wrap-a-round skirt and a white blouse. On the sleeve was a blue-and-yellow emblem with words written in French which said: "NEW Missions; Haiti—Hope in God." Cindy, Diane, and I planned to wear the uniforms most of the time to look more professional, especially whenever we did city business.

Although Charlie was with us, Timothy wouldn't be flying in for another week, giving us a little time to set up. Accompanying Timothy would be my father, nephew, and four others who planned to help with the first construction.

Our truck was still sitting in customs, tangled in red tape. Therefore, when we arrived in Port-au-Prince, we rented one. But because of the crowded road conditions and the rutted three and a half miles of dirt roads leading up to our property, the 20-mile trip took more than two hours.

We pulled up to our property, and I could see that it would require a lot of work. Swampy and wet, it was filled with jungle brush four to six feet tall. Since nothing had been able to grow on it except coconut trees, the Haitians in the surrounding villages felt the land was evil and were unwilling to set foot on it. I was also told that the Leogane area had more voodoo than anywhere else in Haiti. And since Haiti had more voodoo than anywhere else in the world, I knew we had a spiritual battle on our hands.

The land, however, did have its advantages. Situated on the beautiful Bay of LaGonave, it was three and a half miles from the highway, allowing us plenty of privacy. The property ran along the ocean front, and its emerald blue waters lapped our shore.

We set up our tents near the stream on a flat grassy part of the land. Soon we met the caretaker of our property who was responsible to the chief of our section. He was an older man named San Louis, and his eyes were set deep in a wrinkled, smiling face. Twenty years earlier, a man from Port-au-Prince had told San Louis that he had a vision of white people coming across the ocean and living on this land to help his people. As a result, San Louis received us with open arms, already informing the other villagers that we were good people.

That afternoon I gazed at the tiny village of Bord Mer—no more than 100 feet away. Beneath the radiant azure sky, rows of mud huts, roughly the size of a two-man tent, with dirt floors and thatched roofs, dotted the landscape. The villagers were poor. They didn't own the land their huts were built on, but paid a small rent instead.

Beyond Bord Mer, a half mile away, was another village called Neply, where 1,000 more Haitians lived. A stream ran alongside both villages next to the bumpy dirt road which went out to the main highway. Several women were bent over, washing their clothes and dishes. Cows, goats and pigs occasionally came to drink from the water. Soon I discovered that it was the same water the Haitians themselves used for drinking.

The stream that ran through our property, went through a village before it got to us. Now that it was early afternoon, the water was already full of murk. Since we had no good water supply ourselves, I realized we would have to get up early to have clean water for bathing. Fortunately, a nearby mission had agreed to let us draw water from their well to get drinking water. But since the mission was seven and a half miles away and we wouldn't always have access to a vehicle, we would have to use our water sparingly. To get food and other supplies in Port-au-Prince, we decided to rent a vehicle for a couple of days each week.

As I watched several naked toddlers frolicking in the mud with goats and chickens nearby, I cringed. It wasn't the animals that bothered me as much as the children's bloated bellies, orange hair, and runny noses—all signs of malnutrition.

I looked away and closed my eyes, not wanting to see one more hungry child. Vainly, I tried to comfort myself in the fact that soon they would be fed; soon they would be in school.

Since this was Haiti's "winter" season, a tropical breeze swept through our property, bringing a refreshing cool. Yet by 5:00 P.M., it was beginning to turn dark. Quickly, we hung our royal blue banner between two palm trees. Written across it in gold lettering were the words, written in French: "Haiti—Hope in God." Next, we sat in a circle, holding flashlights and pounding a stake into the ground, proclaiming that Satan had no power over us and that God was the victor.

Later that night, I lay on my hard tent floor with just a light blanket over me, trying to sleep. Then I stopped moving and listened. In the distance, I could hear voodoo drums, and then another sound—like that of a hooting owl. I wrapped my blanket snugly around me, and tried to shut out the uncomfortable sounds, refusing to be afraid. For I was finally on the mission field and finally able to fulfill the call of God on my life.

I thought of the banner we put up a few hours earlier, telling the Haitians to hope in God. Yet I knew that the books I read concerning this country had said that the conditions here were hopeless; Haiti was past rescuing. I thought of the Scripture found in Romans 15:13, and I made it my prayer for them: "May the God of hope fill you with all joy and peace as you trust in him, so that you may overflow with hope by the power of the Holy Spirit" (NIV). With God, I believed, there was hope for these people.

"People of Bord Mer and Neply," I whispered. "Hope in God. Hope in God...."

Somehow, God would have to make a way for these suffering individuals—and for us.

Chapter 11

Life in Rural Haiti

After ten days, I was still adjusting to my new environment. Life in the States now seemed like a distant memory each morning when the rooster crowed before dawn, waking me from an uncomfortable sleep on my new rag-filled Haitian mattress. I decided that the Haitians must have stuffed it with bones as well; something inside it was always poking me at night.

School started the second week we arrived. Forty children gathered under the palm trees where our banner flew high and where we held our Sunday morning services. While the children sat on wooden planks supported by cement blocks and used tables made out of shipping pallets, Cindy and Diane taught them Bible stories, songs, and some letters and numbers.

Before the children left each day, Cindy and Diane made sure to feed them a high protein meal, aware that they were almost always hungry. Typically in a Haitian home, the father and anyone else who worked ate first—then the mother, and finally the children. Often, by the time the children got their portion, there was little left.

Timothy, my father, and five other volunteers had just arrived, laden with treats of cheese and chocolate. It was good to see Timothy, carrying his school books with him to study and keep up with his American classmates. And now, along with our son Charlie, the rest of the group was ready to begin construction of our community house. We had hired 15 Haitian men to clear the thorny jungle brush, and George had purchased some of the necessary building materials.

From the start we worked to make life more comfortable for everyone. For one thing, a pastor's wife who had joined us was not at all happy about our toilet facilities—a row in the sugarcane fields somewhere. So George bought a 50-gallon barrel drum and a ceramic toilet, which he connected to a pipe and ran into the ground. Then, after filling the drum with stream water, he placed a bucket beside it which could be used to flush the water down the toilet. A privacy wall was fashioned around the toilet by using woven coconut palm leaves held up by sticks and tied with wire.

Since we had no refrigeration, we kept large quantities of dry food available to cook on our kerosene stove. All of us lived on a simple diet of pancakes, rice, beans and vegetables, avoiding meats and local eggs. Unfortunately, even the simplest meal took hours to prepare, especially since we kept having problems with our stove. Finally, a visiting pastor bought us a two-burner propane gas unit which proved far more reliable.

Cindy and Diane not only taught school but worked long hours each day in the clinic where patients lined up before dawn, many holding swollen, fevered babies. Fresh-squeezed orange juice or a mild protein drink was distributed to those who were severely malnourished. For the more seriously ill, the nurses made "hut" calls, running from place to place until they were exhausted. Sometimes when they saw a baby with a high fever and admonished the mother to get the baby to the clinic, the mother often responded by saying, "Si bondye vle" (If it's God's will), the baby will die. This fatalistic attitude on the part of the Haitians was one we hoped God would eventually change.

Another strange custom was that Haitian mothers never nursed their babies for three days after delivery; instead, a *La Lok* was performed to clean out their digestive systems. This involved putting oil and spices down the newborn's throat. Sprinkling ashes over the baby's cut umbilical cord in a voodoo ritual was another common practice. Even older people—plagued with worms or stomach problems—often had a *La Lok* performed.

There were many infant deaths, usually the result of diarrhea, the number one killer in the country. Many Haitian mothers, after noticing that Charlie bought dried fish packed in small wooden boxes, requested the empty boxes to bury their babies.

∞ ∞ ∞ ∞ ∞

I rubbed my eyes and forced myself to my feet. Soon George and I were traipsing down to the stream dressed in our bathing suits, to take a cold bath before the water became murky again from women washing their clothes upstream. We planned to go into Port-au-Prince to order a few more construction supplies and to pick up food. But now, since we no longer had the luxury of a vehicle—renting one only when our son, Charlie, volunteered to retrieve water and other heavy items—we had to be selective in what we bought. We knew we would have to carry everything in our backpacks on our return trip.

After our early morning stream bath, George and I headed for the main highway, three and a half miles away. Once we reached it, we planned on taking a tap-tap—a colorfully-painted carnival-like vehicle—that was used as a form of public transportation. As we maneuvered our way along the uneven dirt road filled with potholes, our pace was slow and unsteady. As we walked, we passed several half-starved cows, horses, and goats, tied up because there were no fences anywhere. Neither was there good pasture land.

We had covered only two and a half miles in an hour of walking when a Haitian man approached us. Speaking loudly, he mocked us in Creole: "They'll never let you on the tap-tap. And if they do, you'll have to pay a lot of money." On and on he taunted us as we quickened our stride and tried to ignore him. Part of me wanted to fight back with words. Instead, I forced my anger down, trying not to tarnish my missionary image. George however, stared straight ahead, seemingly able to ignore the annoyance. This man kept up with us, like a pesky fly we couldn't shake.

After we finally flagged down a tap-tap, the man encouraged the driver to charge us more. By then, George and I were too tired to care, hardly noticing that the vehicle was overcrowded and in terrible disrepair. We were jammed in like cattle, fighting the overpowering stench of body odor, exacerbated by the heat. My body twisted in different directions as I tried to make myself comfortable. Then, the tap-tap stopped and a woman carrying live chickens took a seat beside me. I could feel the fear rising to my throat. When the chicken feathers touched my legs, I recoiled in horror. By the time George and I arrived in the city an hour later, my nerves were shot and my body was numb and aching.

The city of Port-au-Prince was just as much of a nightmare. Disorder and filth were everywhere—even the courtyards of the government offices were littered with garbage. George hated the chaos and endless waiting, but by the end of the day he managed to order the construction supplies he needed. Meanwhile, I picked up medical supplies, sugar, jelly, and a jar of peanut butter. I also picked up a frozen chicken and a dozen eggs to help boost our morale. After loading our backpacks, we headed for home.

One and a half hours later, weary and exhausted, we stepped off the tap-tap and started the three-and-a-half-mile walk back to our mission. As I trudged along the dusty, hot road beside George, feeling a trickle of sweat move down my brow, I prayed that someone might come by and give us a ride.

Just then, I noticed an old man in a wooden cart, pulled by two oxen in the field next to us. Immediately he motioned for us to climb up. Even though the ride was jostled, it gave me the relief I needed.

One mile from our mission property, the man let us off and we resumed our journey on foot. Passing by the village of Neply, I studied the women, noticing how tall and erect they walked with an elegant grace to their step. I knew that their posture wasn't a result of their high self-esteem, but rather one that had been perfected through years of carrying everything on their heads. In Haiti, every woman was known by her husband's name, having no identity of her own—a reflection of the position she had in their society. I was already being referred to as "Madam George."

I watched a woman grate coconut to make milk to add to her family's meager dinner. Next to her, a pot of food was cooking on top of three rocks, as wood burned underneath this common type of "stove." A few chickens darted nearby, waiting for any possible coconut droppings to eat. I soon discovered that nothing was ever wasted in Haiti; even banana skins were saved for the goats.

Two naked toddlers played quietly beside their mother, waiting for their first meal of the day. A mother often pacified her children's hunger with pieces of sugarcane, hoping to put off their meal for as long as possible. If they ate too early, they would be too hungry to sleep at night. Only when the children really started crying from hunger would the mother bring out the cooking pot, causing them to settle down. Then the children realized that they would eventually be fed, even though they usually waited another hour or two until their food was cooked.

I shook my head, wondering how long an American child would last. From what I observed, American children didn't wait well and often were ungrateful for what they were served.

By the time we arrived back at our camp, my chicken was thawed and dripping, and George and I were exhausted. Experiencing a lifestyle similar to the Haitians was beginning to give me a lot more compassion and understanding for them.

I would soon discover, however, that it would take more than a little sweat to develop any kind of real bonding with the Haitian women.

Chapter 12

Faced with Reality

The bright sun shone directly overhead as George and I entered the village of Neply to do some visitation. There was a spring in my step as I walked, for I was eager to befriend these Haitian women before I told them about Jesus. During the last month, I was so busy cooking, overseeing the team, and doing administrative work that I had little time to get to know them. Memories of the wonderful relationships I had with the precious women in India came flooding back. My heart warmed as I pictured them—their open, hungry faces welcoming me, ready and receptive to all I had to share. Maybe, I hoped, my relationship with the women here would be just as spontaneous and enriching. And since we were already feeding and educating their children...

Just then, I felt someone pulling on the back of my dress, shaking me out of my reverie. Spinning around, I noticed a large-boned, toothless woman scowling at me. "Give me your dress!" she demanded. Before I could respond, two other women rushed to my side. "I'll come to church, but I don't have any shoes," the youngest complained. "Give me some shoes."

"Why don't you ever give us anything?" the older one questioned, her mouth filled with crooked, stained teeth.

Deeply offended, I tried to control my anger. I was a pastor's wife for 25 years and everyone had always been nice to me; I even had women who wanted to model their lives after mine. When I reached out in love, women had always loved me back. But here I was, feeding and educating their children, and all they would do was beg, taunt, and insult me. I was hurt. Offended. At that moment, I didn't care if they ever heard about Jesus.

I stifled a sharp retort, but George lost his patience. "I'm not having any of your kids in my school," he snapped. "Don't ask for anything again. You're not going to treat my wife that way."

Although it felt good to have George come to my defense, I cringed at his words. Not only did I realize he would never carry out his threat, but I knew he would soon regret his response. Fielding insults was sometimes the small cost of being a missionary.

As we made our way to our sponsored child's home, my heart felt heavy, frustrated by this first attempt to befriend the Haitians. At least now I had a better understanding of why it had been so important for God to deal with me concerning my past resentments and insecurities. How much more difficult it would have been if I hadn't let go of those things and found my security in Him.

Fortunately, the rest of the afternoon went smoothly as George and I visited a few huts where we were well received. I kept my eye out for children Timothy's age I could research for my thesis. As soon as the villagers realized what I needed, they clamored around me, trying to get their own children selected in the hopes of gaining something in return.

Later that week, I selected 20 children to observe. I wanted to learn how they helped their parents. Did they walk to the stream to get water? Did they wash clothes? Fetch wood?

It didn't take long to find out that the Haitian children did all these things and more. Soon I was measuring the distance from one mud hut to the stream to see how far a child had to carry water. Then I weighed the water to see how heavy it was. I discovered that a 10-year-old child could completely care for an infant, build a fire, make the meals, clean a hut, and ride a donkey.

Whenever I asked the children questions, the whole village turned out to watch the show. Even the mothers seemed to enjoy the attention their children were getting, easing my discomfort a little. Yet they didn't really seem to want a relationship, they just seemed to *want*—period. Even after I measured how far their children carried water, a woman wanted to know if I was going to provide plumbing for her hut.

It became evident to me that I knew the heartbeat of the American women but not that of the Haitian women. I had compassion for their circumstances, especially since we were living as they were. I also knew what it was like to walk in the hot sun and live without electricity and other conveniences. But I didn't have the constant fear of starvation.

At some level, I knew a bonding was taking place with the Haitians in general. But the women? Maybe they didn't understand that I wasn't just another rich American, that I had feelings, too. Although some of the women had responded to me with consideration and respect, right now I was feeling like a ball of string being batted about by a lot of insensitive kittens.

I knew my attitude was wrong. How could God possibly use me to touch these women if I kept allowing myself to be offended? In college I was taught to try to see the good in a culture; any necessary changes should only be brought about after relationships were established. Yet I was painfully aware that I still hadn't learned how to listen to the needs of the Haitian people without becoming offended myself.

George had his frustrations as well. Unlike our son, Charlie, who was gentle and patient by nature, George often felt exasperated. Once when we were passing through Bord Mer—the village right next to us—he noticed some toddlers waddling in the mud next to two large pigs. Their parents stood a few feet away, completely unconcerned.

"You people are letting your kids live with the pigs," George complained. "And there's garbage everywhere." It was true. Disorder was all around us. Over and over, George admonished them to change their ways, feeling it was important that someone tell them.

But George wasn't unkind and had a deep love for the Haitian people. He was taking care of Sovy Louis, a young boy Timothy's age. When the boy first visited our tent site, his head was full of lice and his skin dry and cracked—signs of third-degree malnutrition. Every day George fed him and scrubbed the boy's head until the lice had disappeared and he was well again. He then made sure that Sovy was attending our school.

Some of the other missionaries were also bonding well with the children. One day, during an afternoon visit, I saw Cindy—a sensitive, outgoing woman of average height and light-brown hair—with a whole flock of 11- and 12-year-old girls who followed her around while she made hut calls. I watched as she reached inside her bag and pulled out a package of chocolate chips. She handed them out for all the girls to taste. Little did I realize that this same group of girls would eventually become some of our most faithful and dedicated followers of the Lord Jesus.

Just then, 8-year-old Manise, our sponsored child, came running towards me, pulling a crying toddler along with her. I noticed she was wearing the same lime-green polyester dress that she always wore with the interfacing hanging out. I also observed the obvious differences in her appearance now that she was being fed a healthy diet: Her orange hair was turning to brown and, despite her shyness, she was no longer listless and sad. Yet I noticed that the little girl beside her, not more than 18 months old, had all the familiar features of malnutrition.

Manise explained that the little girl was her cousin, Rosita. Then she cried, "Grangou, grangou," letting me know her cousin was hungry. I surmised that Rosita had probably just been weaned, which was usually the time when serious malnutrition developed.

"Please," Manise continued, pulling on my sleeve in the direction of our mission, "don't you have any milk for her?"

I squatted down and reached out my hand towards the little girl, but she backed away. White people were still an oddity, something to be feared. Then, in my best Creole, I invited Manise and Rosita back to the mission.

They followed me to the clinic where I mixed up dry milk with good drinking water and gave Manise a quart of milk for her cousin. By the time they left, I had produced two happy children.

Unfortunately, I realized that this was only a drop in the bucket—there were so many hungry children that age. As soon as possible, George and I hoped to start a mother-infant program to provide the proper nutrition toddlers needed after they were weaned. But right now we felt overwhelmed. How do you feed one child and not the next? How do you feed the children and not the parents? Over and over, we had to ask God for the grace to concentrate on feeding the 40 children who were enrolled in our school.

Even Timothy had a hard time coping with the poverty. Each day, as he sat hunched over an old wooden table under a coconut palm tree doing his school work, the dark, hungry faces of the children gathered around him. Since they had never seen so many school books before, they stared at them in fascination.

It wasn't long before Timothy befriended many of them, even giving them a few Sunday school lessons through the help of an interpreter. But their poverty and lack of schooling had already made a huge impression on him as I thought it surely must on everyone. However, an incident occurred within a few weeks that made me realize that not everyone chooses to see the poverty.

It happened in Port-au-Prince, where I was spending the day at the library of the United States Agency for International Development (U.S.A.I.D.). As soon as I arrived, I scoured their books, looking for any information that might be useful for my thesis. But there appeared to be nothing on child labor in Haiti.

After a fruitless, frustrating day, I chatted with the Haitian librarian there, explaining some of the suffering and starvation I encountered.

She gave me a blank stare. "I never see the sick," she explained. "I never see the hungry."

My mouth dropped open. Even in Port-au-Prince, poverty was all around. Yet, for the first time, I realized that we must want to see the poor. Just as Jesus had to be moved with compassion, so did we. Otherwise, we might just see a need and simply move on.

After that eye-opening encounter, I met a Haitian named Jean-Claude at U.S.A.I.D. who worked on development projects. Eventually, he helped me make a few contacts with some of the agencies that distribute food. Even though some of them got as many as 1,000 applications a year, the contacts eventually proved very helpful in getting us the assistance we needed.

As I concentrated on issues of nutrition, George oversaw the physical work that went on in the mission, praying continually for wisdom. Right after we arrived, he had hired San Louis—the previous caretaker of our property whom we soon called Papa—to be our foreman. He proved invaluable, protecting us from several Haitians who tried to exploit us, and finding us honest help instead. His daughter-in-law,

Rosette—Manise's mother—was hired to wash clothes for us as well.

Each morning at 7:00 A.M., San Louis sounded the whistle for the men to begin working. After six weeks the outside and inside walls of the mission building, as well as the plumbing, had all been completed. Work was starting on the roof.

Papa even helped us in our relationship with the voodoo leaders, telling them we were sent here by the good God—someone they all believed in—to do a good work for their people. As a result, they rarely felt threatened by our presence. Had they been, the voodoo priests could have easily crippled our efforts, since they controlled their people by fear and could have encouraged them to stay away. Instead the voodoo priest put his children in our school.

While the physical work continued on our property, we received word that a new 24-foot diesel engine boat was enroute to Haiti—a gift from one of our friends in Massachusetts. Our son, Charlie, who had taken a few navigational courses in the past, was eager to be its new captain. Soon he was taking this vessel to bring the Gospel and medical relief to the small isolated villages along the bay, where so many fishermen struggled to survive. Since none of them could afford a power boat and could only row so far, they never threw any fish, even the tiniest, back into the water. That little fish provided just enough food to keep one of them going for one more day.

After two and a half months, our first building wasfinally up—a multipurposed U-shaped community house. It contained a kitchen, office, bathroom, clinic room, and housing facilities for our missionaries. The front deck would also be used to hold our church meetings. We moved in immediately, even before the windows and doors were in place.

Two weeks later, George and I had to leave. Charlie would remain behind with Curt, Cindy, John, and Diane who would stay on until their one-year commitment had ended.

Before we returned home, I noticed that the change in our school children was already quite pronounced. Instead of orange hair, infected skin, and bloated bellies, they had strong little bodies topped with black shiny hair—and there was a new energy to their step. We had hired several Haitian school teachers for them from Port-au-Prince. Therefore, eyes that were once dull and hollow, lacking mental stimulation, now shined with new hope. The children were responding to God's Word.

It was with mixed feelings that George and I headed for the airport to return home to Worcester. Although we were looking forward to seeing Mary Ann, George, Jr., and our church congregation, there was still so much that needed to be done in Haiti. Despite the obstacles, George and I were thriving on the challenge of living in Haiti and seeing God at work. We were climbing a new mountain—a much taller one than we first had realized—and we were still a long distance from reaching the top.

Once we were back, it was especially wonderful to be reunited with our daughter. Unfortunately, it had been a tough three months for her, living at the community house. Not only did she experience little privacy, but she had a hard time relating to the other women at the facility.

Mary Ann immediately moved back home with us and life returned to normal. Yet none of us could forget our experiences. Once, when Timothy stood in front of our church to share about the Haitian children, he suddenly burst into tears. A moment later, he bolted from the platform pulpit, too overcome with emotion to continue. Memories of those little hungry faces—many of them now his friends—were simply too overwhelming.

George, too, carried the message by speaking at different churches, telling congregations about our vision for Haiti and trying to drum up support. I also shared my experiences, while trying to finish up my thesis for my master's degree. Two months after our return to Worcester, Timothy graduated easily from the seventh grade.

While we were home we continued to hear good progress reports from Haiti. More than 500 patients were being treated each month in the clinic. And, after five months, our 1970 Dodge pickup truck and an 8K generator had been released from Haitian customs, although it ended up costing us several thousand dollars. It was worth it; the prices would have been doubled had they been purchased in Haiti.

On July 11—six months after our mission first started—we received formal recognition with the government of Haiti, allowing us to own property in the name of NEW Missions and to be at liberty to function freely throughout the country. We felt especially pleased with this news after several other missionaries informed us that it had taken them years to receive recognition from the government.

Meanwhile, Charlie was blossoming in Haiti, helping to run the school and feeding programs. He had also established excellent relationships with the agencies distributing food; his gentle, patient manner was a big help in dealing with them. Already, the Haitians in the area were saying that because we were feeding their children, there was enough food now for everyone, and no one was starving to death anymore.

George and I continued fund-raising for Haiti as well as handling much of the administration work. One hundred sixty-one children were already enrolled for school for the fall of 1983. We felt pulled in two directions, trying to run a mission and a church simultaneously.

We knew we couldn't continue this way indefinitely. Our mission was growing constantly, demanding more and more time. Soon we were praying about whether we should move to Haiti permanently. Yet one of our senior elders, who had been discipled by George and was like one of our sons, doubted we would seriously consider such a move. He reminded us that we went from living on $50 a week in a run-down building and a handful of members to a flourishing church of middle-class professionals.

It was true. It had taken us 16 years to get to a place where we were no longer struggling: We had a nice salary and excellent benefits, a beautiful 10-room Victorian home, a sailboat at a mooring in Newport harbor, and a wonderful ministry. Wasn't it foolish to consider giving it all up? Besides, now that I had been to Haiti, I wondered how effectively God could use me there. I had bonded with the Haitians in general, but I couldn't seem to break through to the women. It had been so easy in India. Why was I missing the mark with them?

I didn't know the answers. I only knew that my own missionary call kept tugging at my heart, beckoning me to return.

One evening, after George and I retired for the night, sleep eluded me as my thoughts buzzed around and around in my head. The faces of the Haitians loomed before me— their hungry bellies, their bodies devoid of energy, and their dull, sunken eyes. But most of all it was their souls I saw— hurting, empty, and waiting—waiting for someone to tell them about the unconditional love of Jesus.

Chapter 13

Learning to Love

January, 1984—one year after George and I had first come to work in Haiti for three months—we were back again for another tour of duty. While George oversaw the construction work, I planned to help one of our young church members, Lauretta, with a mother-infant program she started in the nearby village of Neply. Each day, while working out of a small cement house, she fed 130 toddlers; if the mothers were nursing, she fed the mother instead. I could hardly wait to help her. I was sure the mothers and I would become good friends once I started giving them devotionals and helping to distribute the food.

It was wonderful to see the children in our school wearing their new uniforms—the girls in yellow-and-white-checkered dresses and the boys in tan shorts. Their dark faces glowed as they carried their books to school each day, which was now being held in four large thatched houses which held 40 students each. Unfortunately, on rainy days, the water poured through the straw roof, making the benches wet and the ground muddy. Eventually we hoped to build four classrooms made of cement.

The classrooms were located across from our community house, which was now finished. A generator had also been installed, giving us electricity. We also purchased a stove and a refrigerator, which we desperately needed to keep our food and medicines cold. Despite the fact that we still had no running water or telephone, and that it was almost impossible to leave the mission during the rainy season because of the poor road conditions, none of our missionaries or visiting teams seemed anxious about the living conditions.

Although I bonded with most of the Haitians, I had a hard time feeling welcomed by Pierre, the Chief of Police in our area, who was considered a powerful man. Tall and heavyset, with deep eyes, he checked up on any foreigners in his domain, taking down our passport numbers and making sure our status was up-to-date. Living just two miles down the road, he was also responsible for handling any disputes between the Haitians and us. Pierre also had to write a letter to the Haitian government explaining why we were here and what we were doing—and he didn't seem to trust us.

Then our relationship turned a corner. I showed him a photograph of my four children. Then I told him that I had four other children in heaven. A large smile crossed his face as he explained that his wife had also lost four children.

From that moment on, our relationship warmed. He seemed to realize that I, too, had experienced suffering— and that maybe I wasn't such a bad person after all.

The mother-infant program provided more of a challenge than I thought. In the midst of screaming babies and toddlers who were terrified of white people, I struggled in my broken Creole to give the women instructions to line up for their food.

Soon it was obvious that just getting them to form a line and come forward when their names were called was a monumental task. They felt if they didn't push and shove, they wouldn't get anything. And when I called their names, they often let someone else answer, or changed their names completely to keep me off balance.

I was especially frustrated when a woman told me she was Mona; the day before she had been Lucy. I could see the other women smirking as my cheeks felt hot and red. These women didn't want order since they hoped for the chance to trick us and get a second bowl. They also hoped their misbehavior would force us to let them take their food home. But we knew if we let that happen, the food would be shared with others. Finally, Lauretta and I memorized the women by the dresses they wore, which were always the same, day after day.

Because I knew these women had no church background, I couldn't give them a Bible study like I did in the States. Instead, I used simple illustrations to get my message across. I told them about the roll that would be called in heaven and how our names were written on it. I also hoped it would encourage them to be more honest about their real names when Lauretta and I called them to come forward for food.

After my devotional, I passed out face cloths—something I knew they would like. Immediately chaos erupted.

One of the women yelled, "I didn't get one."

"I didn't either."

As I started to hand a face cloth to each of them, another woman grabbed them out of my hand.

Where did these women learn their manners? I wanted to know. But then I caught myself. These were women who couldn't read or write, who lived in mud huts and who had no contact with the outside world. They were afraid—afraid that if they didn't grab and claw and beg, there would be nothing left for them. Their survival instinct was what dictated their actions, and I realized it was going to take time to develop the kind of trust between us that was needed. Although I didn't realize it at the time, I needed to learn a few more lessons about the Haitian women themselves before I was able to truly understand and love them as I should.

Soon an incident occurred that helped me towards that goal. It was late one evening when I was summoned to see Jeannine, a woman who lived in the local neighborhood, known as Bord Mer. Jeannine lived in a tiny two-room mud hut with several children; the fathers had all deserted her. Fortunately, her children were attending our school.

When I arrived at her hut, the door was surrounded by sticks and branches to keep people out. I called Jeannine's name, and she appeared in the doorway. A tall, stocky woman, her face and arms were black and blue and she was holding her head, obviously in pain. It was apparent she had been beaten.

Her story spilled out. She explained that her mother had died and left the mud hut to her. But her uncle, feeling that the hut should be his, had beaten her, demanding that she move out.

These were circumstances that were all too common in Haiti. Our nurses had told me that several village women were being physically abused and were coming to our clinic bruised, cut, and bleeding. But this was the first time I actually saw the abuse myself. I had also heard that Haitian men often compared their women to a shellfish known as lambi. Before they cooked the fish, it had to be beaten to tenderize it. They explained that for women to be really tender toward them, they had to beat them in the same way. In other words, they felt it was normal and good to beat their women.

The closest pharmacy was an eight-mile walk, so I went to our clinic and gave Jeannine a few painkillers. Gratefully, she accepted.

During the next hour I lay awake, unable to get Jeannine out of my mind. Finally, I slipped out of bed, opened my cupboard and pulled out a can of cocoa. After mixing it up with some milk and lots of sugar—Haitians love things sweet—I returned to Jeannine's mud hut.

The painkillers and cocoa changed our relationship from that evening on. The incident also helped me understand the importance of reaching out in practical ways to these suffering women. Years later, I realized that small acts of kindness were the real cement that would finally bond us deeply together.

The children moved me even further toward building relationships with our Haitian neighbors. One was a 10-year-old boy from Neply named Rodrigues, a student at our school. One day, after becoming sick with dysentery and digestive problems, he was seen at our clinic.

Cindy—who was back again for a short time—told me to take him to the hospital. She would also be accompanying us with a baby girl who was severely dehydrated and whose lips were quivering—a sign that death was imminent unless she received treatment immediately.

While George drove the truck, I sat beside him, holding Rodrigues in my arms. Ten years old, but weighing just 32 pounds, he was completely emaciated—his arms and legs nothing but bone and a little hanging skin. Although he appeared conscious, his eyes bulged as he gazed at me. Caressing Rodrigues' face, I tried to make him as comfortable as possible. I thought of my own son, Timothy, who was the same age. Over and over again, as I told Rodrigues how much Jesus loved him, I cried out to God to spare his life.

When we reached the hospital, Cindy left the baby in one of the wards. Then she rushed down the street to a pharmacy to buy an IV for the baby and some gastro-intestinal medicine for Rodrigues. Not only is emergency care nonexistent in Haiti, but the hospital does not provide the medicine or food. Recently, we heard that one boy had starved to death because the family had failed to come and give him food.

A few minutes after Cindy had returned from the pharmacy, I was making Rodrigues as comfortable as possible in one of the other rooms when she bolted through the door. "It's too late!" Cindy wailed. "The baby's dead!"

Pattering over, I put my arm around her. "You did all you could," I responded, trying to bring her some comfort. But at that moment, I knew it was to no avail. Words could never ease her heartache at a time like this.

Cindy gave Rodrigues his medicine as tears spilled from her eyes. At least Rodrigues, although delirious, looked like he might make it. After saying goodbye, Cindy and I returned to the mission with George.

Hours later we received word that Rodrigues had died as well.

The next day, I went to Neply, where Rodrigues' body, clothed in his school uniform, lay on a straw mat inside his mud hut. I shook my head. It all seemed so senseless.

A few days after Rodrigues was buried, the director of our school approached me. He explained that a new boy named Michelet had shown up wearing one of our uniforms. The boy had told him he was Rodrigues' brother—and that he was attending our school in his brother's place.

The director went on to say that Michelet had been living in Port-au-Prince. Although he was only 11—a year older than Rodrigues—he had no opportunity to go to school there. So, after attending his brother's funeral, Michelet had stripped Rodrigues of his uniform and put it on, hoping to gain admittance into our school program.

The director wanted to know if we should let him stay. Our school was already stretched to capacity.

"Yes," I decided. "Let him stay."

The director walked off, and I couldn't help but be amazed at the Haitians' ability to survive and move on. Even in death, I realized, nothing was sacred—not even the clothes you were buried in.

As our month-long stay in Haiti came to an end, we found it even harder to leave. Our love and vision for the Haitian people had become even greater than before.

∞ ∞ ∞ ∞ ∞

Three months after returning home, George and I took a walk around a park, just four blocks from our house. It was springtime and the lovely smell of lilacs permeated the air. As much as we loved our church and family, we knew that our hearts were no longer in the States. As the work in Haiti kept expanding, we realized it was time to make a decision.

Stopping near a pond filled with ducks, George stared at me, slipping his arm around my waist. We had spent a lot of time praying over our next step. Finally George spoke up: "Let's go for it."

Nodding my head in agreement, my eyes shone with happiness. It had been seven years since I had been to India, and now I was going to the mission field permanently. Once the dream had seemed impossible. Now it was finally, unbelievably, happening!

In June, George resigned from his pastorate after 25 years of ministry. We visited churches all over New England, trying to raise funds for our mission and for our own support as well. Fortunately, we still owned a three-family apartment building in Worcester, enabling us to use the rent money to help put our children through college, plus furnish a few of our own needs while we were gone.

Other things quickly fell into place. Several well-meaning Christians offered to buy our home and furniture from us. However, we decided to keep the place so our children could have somewhere they could call home. We also moved our mission office from the church into our home so we would have no rental expenses. George, Jr. planned to oversee our office while continuing to work towards his business degree at nearby Clark University. My mother also agreed to pitch in, and she found other volunteers to help with various administrative tasks. Mary Ann would be attending the University of Massachusetts in

Amherst. That left Charlie, who planned to remain with us in Haiti, and Timothy, who continued his school work through correspondence.

On October 30, I was on my knees at midnight, praising God in our small mission office at our home. People were giving generously to our mission, and Haitian children were being sponsored. How grateful I felt. Yet after fifteen minutes, a terrible fear took hold. Shifting my thoughts to all the wonderful things that were happening in Haiti, I still couldn't seem to shake the cold chill that had settled over me.

Thirty minutes later, I received a phone call from Charlie in Haiti. He explained that two of our short-term missionaries had returned home from the city at dusk and had hit a truck parked on the highway without any lights. Not only was our vehicle totaled, but Lauretta—whom I assisted with the mother-infant program—had been pinned under the dashboard. Our driver had managed to get her out of the vehicle and lay her on the side of the highway while he ran to the nearest mission for help. As Lauretta lay there with broken bones and cuts from shattered glass, some Haitians approached in a tap-tap. Two of them managed to carry her on board to take her to the hospital. Yet as soon as she explained that she didn't have any money with her, they removed her from the tap-tap and placed her on the side of the road. A short time later, our driver managed to return with help and get her to the hospital. Eventually Lauretta was flown to Boston where she was hospitalized with a broken knee and fractured rib. She soon made a full recovery.

Through the generosity of an older widow, we were able to purchase a white Toyota pickup truck. Although it wasn't air conditioned, it was reliable and used diesel fuel, which would be a great money-saver. We thought our troubles were behind us, but that minor incident was a forerunner of difficulties ahead. Soon I would realize that we needed all our years of training and preparation in the ministry for the challenges in our future.

Chapter 14

A New Level of Bonding

It was the day before Christmas. George, Timothy, and I had been living permanently in Haiti for several weeks, and our son Charlie was finishing his second year. As happy as I was to be back, I felt saddened that there was no tinsel, no Christmas trees, no presents, or no special food for the villagers. So today, on Christmas Eve, I set out our two-burner propane gas unit on our mission deck, and made as many donuts as I could—dipped in chocolate frosting and loaded with coconut, fresh from our trees. Then I handed them out to every Haitian who passed by.

I headed for the village, loaded with donuts and a few presents. Ducking into the mud hut of a mother I knew, I saw 3-year-old Tanya fast asleep on a thin mattress. Quietly, I tucked a doll under her covers beside her so she would discover the gift in the morning. Then I visited Manise's home, bringing her and her family food, clothing, and a little money.

Later I walked to Bord Mer with a small gift from one of the children's sponsors. The family had four girls and one boy, and now the mother was pregnant again. Their 5-year-old girl, Sherline, was handicapped and couldn't walk.

Stepping into the mud hut to see if the girl was home, my eyes fastened on Sherline, lying to my right. Covered with flies and completely emaciated, her mouth was dry and cracked—signs that she was starving to death.

It was obvious her mother had made a conscious decision to let the child die. Yet rather than being appalled, I realized that when someone is struggling just to keep their healthy children alive, the burden of a handicapped child can become overwhelming. Now she was pregnant again and probably felt she could no longer care for Sherline.

Wasting no time, I turned to the mother and explained, "If you want me to find a home to care for Sherline, I will."

The mother nodded, yet didn't seem to have the emotional strength to bring her to our clinic. Quickly, the grandmother volunteered to carry her for me.

A few minutes later our nurses were working on the little girl, pumping formula into her and cleaning her up. Fortunately, we weren't too late. After she was restored to health, we were able to get her into an orphanage 10 miles away.

During the next year our mission expanded rapidly. Soon we had children from eight surrounding villages enrolled in our mission school at Bord Mer, bringing the total to 524. Recently, three more missionaries had joined us. One of the young women, whose name was Kim, was appalled at the conditions she saw in the village of LaSalle, just a mile from us. The village was full of hungry children with runny noses, bloated stomachs, orange hair and eye infections. And there was no church but lots of voodoo in the village.

Soon we hired a man to walk behind Kim, pushing a wheelbarrow full of oatmeal or rice—something that was easy to digest. If a child was sick, Kim did the best she could with a first-aid kit that she carried. After buying straw mats for the children to sit on, she taught them songs and Bible stories.

Eventually a thatched building was erected, serving as both a schoolroom and church building. Two hundred people came to the first church service, and 120 children were already attending the preschool program. We hired someone to begin teaching kindergarten there, and we also built a kindergarten in Neply.

Two acres of land had been purchased in Masson which had access to electricity and well water and was just three miles from our main mission. After constructing a thatched building there, we used it as both a church and school.

The three-and-a-half-mile dirt road leading from our property was also undergoing a change. A Haitian business-man who lived next to our mission had brought in gravel and then graded and rolled it, making it far easier to travel on.

Although our new pickup was holding up well, we were praying for a second vehicle that would be air condi-tioned and could hold more passengers. Without air condi-tioning, we were suffering from exhaust fumes and pollution and were full of soot and dirt every time we went to the city. Because we were forced to keep our windows down, we had been robbed several times. Once, as I put my head out the window to look at an accident, someone grabbed my purse and ran.

As desperately as we needed a second vehicle, we kept putting it off, funneling the money elsewhere. By the end of September, less than a year after we had arrived in Haiti permanently, three concrete school buildings had been constructed. Four other schools also met in thatched build-ings in other villages.

Our biggest need at the mission was a source of clean drinking water. In 1983, we had hired an organization to drill a well at our mission, but their efforts were unsuccess-ful. The water was full of mud and impossible to drink. Now they recommended that we not attempt another well because of what they considered "poor conditions." Also, they felt that since we were so close to the ocean, all we would ever get was salt water.

In place of a well, a pump was placed in the stream that ran alongside our property, and two 300-gallon water tanks were put on a tower. This water was chlorinated, then used for shower and toilet facilities. Although we still didn't have safe drinking and cooking water, we didn't give up hope that someday we would have a well of our own.

During this time, a 25-year-old registered nurse named Kelli joined our mission team. A bold Irish girl with dark brown hair and a pretty face, she quickly became like a second daughter to me. She had heard me speak about our mission at her church in Hyde Park a year earlier. Soon she decided to join us.

Kelli proved invaluable. Once, in the late hours of the night, I was awakened by loud knocking. George got up and lumbered to the door as I rubbed my eyes from sleep. The door flew open, and I saw Manise's stepfather. Quickly, he explained that his wife, Rosette, was in labor, and needed help.

George gave a small groan. There was always someone in labor, it seemed, and the nurses were exhausted, running from hut to hut, delivering baby after baby. We were trying now to teach the Haitians to only send for our nurses after the birth when they were needed to cut the baby's cord.

George turned to me: "Before we wake up a nurse, I'm going to run down on the motorcycle."

A few minutes later, George came bolting through the door. "Honey, the baby's been born, and I think she's in trouble. You need to help."

After waking Kelli, George drove us to Neply, stopping as close to Rosette's hut as possible so that the headlights would illuminate the area, making it possible for us to see.

We entered and saw two women. The older one, holding a kerosene lamp, was crouched over a pale baby girl lying limply on a soiled rag on the mud floor. In her other hand were ashes which she was dropping on the baby's cord, performing voodoo. Several other women joined in the ceremony. I recoiled in horror: The cord, which was still attached to the mother, was wrapped around the baby's neck twice, and the baby wasn't breathing. Nevertheless, Rosette greeted us with a big smile, believing her baby would now be taken care of.

George ordered the women out of the house. "Kelli," he announced, "you work on the baby. Jeanne—you pray." Then he raced outside.

Moments later, I could hear him preaching at the top of his lungs, waking up most of the village: "You people," he exclaimed, "there's a way for a baby to be born—and it's not with hot ashes or voodoo. Jesus wants your children to be healthy." *No wonder Haiti has the highest infant mortality rate in the western hemisphere*, I thought.

While George continued his sermon, I prayed as hard as I could while Kelli worked furiously on the baby, unwrapping the cord from around her neck. Soon we heard the welcome cries of the baby. Kelli proceeded to cut the cord. She picked up the baby, cradling her in her arms. "She's fine," Kelli declared as she handed her to Rosette. Since Kelli had cut the cord, she had the honor of naming the baby. She named her Judy, after one of her best friends who had led her to the Lord.

As we left, I felt so grateful that Kelli had been there. Although I didn't mind praying, I certainly would not have wanted to cut the cord, especially since I had no previous experience.

And then…

One Saturday, close to dinner time, I found myself alone. The other missionaries had gone to the city for a day of rest and relaxation. I remained behind, enjoying a few quiet moments to myself, as well as an opportunity to catch up on my letter writing.

I heard a knock at my door. Opening it, I was greeted by three villagers from Neply, asking for someone to cut the cord of a newborn.

"I'm sorry. All our nurses are gone—and I'm not a nurse."

"We know God is with you. You can do it."

A twinge of panic shot through me. Even though I had watched the nurses cut cords, I had never done one myself. Yet I knew there was no one else.

Mustering my courage, I finally replied, "If I find everything I need, I'll go."

Racing to the clinic, I grabbed a pair of gloves, clips, alcohol, sterile blade, and cotton balls and headed to the village.

Five minutes later, as I stepped inside the packed two-room hut, the air thickened as I fought to breathe. Others stood outside, peering in out of curiosity.

The young mother smiled at me, her face full of trust. Because the white person had arrived, she assumed everything would be fine now: God was with me. Even the baby boy who lay on the mud floor, still attached to his mother by the umbilical cord, waited calmly, without a whimper.

Engulfed by a mob, I felt an almost claustrophobic tension building inside of me. Bathed in a film of sweat, I tried to steady my trembling hands, finally managing to get my sterile gloves on. Then, rummaging through my bag, I took out cotton and alcohol and cleaned the umbilical cord. Next, I took out two plastic clips, placing one an inch from the baby's navel and the other one two inches further down, as I had observed the nurses doing in the past. Although I had no idea why this was necessary, I assumed it was to stop the blood flow so that the baby wouldn't bleed to death.

Then I took a two-inch sterile blade and began cutting the cord. It was real flesh—and it felt tough.

Suddenly my face went white. Blood was squirting from the baby's cord in every direction: One of the clips was obviously defective. I was close to panic. I didn't want to lose my composure, but I could feel my heart beating double-time. Grabbing my bag, I prayed that I brought another clip with me. Frantically, my eyes searched the bottom. Then I saw it—one plastic clip!

Wasting no time, I snatched it up, then discarded the defective clip and replaced it with the new one. *Click!* Immediately, it snapped into place, stopping the blood flow.

A flood of relief washed over me as I finished cutting the cord. The mother looked at me and smiled knowingly.

Before I could relax, however, several old women rushed towards the baby, pushing on his head every which way, trying to "shape" it into a pretty one, as was their custom. Then, three baby hats were put on as tight as possible, as they tried to form the baby's head. Even though I wasn't a nurse, I knew enough to realize that a baby's skull is soft and fragile—not something you're supposed to work on like a piece of putty.

"Stop!" I admonished them, afraid they might cause brain damage.

The women listened, yet what they planned to do next was even more abhorrent. While one of the women grabbed a huge tablespoon and filled it with oil and spices, another one held the baby's mouth open. Instead of having the mother nurse the baby, they were about to perform a *La Lok* to flush out the baby's digestive system.

Fixing my eyes on the mother, I tried to keep my voice steady. "You told me that God was with me, and I could cut the baby's cord. But I will not take responsibility for the life of this baby if you let those women put that oil down his throat. You could kill your baby by doing that."

There was a long pause, then the mother ordered the women to stop. After the baby—whom they already named

Gims Michel—was bathed and dressed, I held him up and said a prayer of blessing and dedication over him. As long as I was there, I was considered the authority—although I have no idea what happened after I left.

Eventually, I ended up cutting a half dozen more cords, allowing me to develop a closer relationship with these women, as well as providing a way of influencing them for Jesus.

Slowly, I was developing a deep bond with the Haitian women. Not only was I reaching out to them in practical ways, but they were beginning to realize that I, too, had experienced the same suffering as they had: Just as a Haitian woman usually loses half of her babies, I had lost half of mine as well. As a result, I could understand their grief and weep with them whenever they experienced a loss of any kind. This enabled me to identify with the Apostle Paul who wrote: "Blessed be the God and Father of our Lord Jesus Christ, the Father of mercies and God of all comfort, who comforts us in all our affliction so that we may be able to comfort those who are in any affliction, with the comfort with which we ourselves are comforted by God" (II Cor. 1:3-4 NAS). This comfort also allowed me to pray that, despite their heartache, the God of hope would fill them with all joy and peace as they trusted in Him (Romans 15:13).

Meanwhile, our nurses began offering prenatal classes to the women. Not only did they teach them to nurse their babies immediately after birth, they also told them of the possible consequences of performing a *La Lok* on a newborn. Eventually the nurses offered a 10-week course in which they trained 18 Haitian midwives in safe, sterile techniques for delivering babies. In the past, unsterile instruments had often been used to cut the umbilical cord, sometimes resulting in tetanus or fatal infections.

After we were in Haiti for just over a year, January 6 marked the third anniversary of our mission. With all of the growth taking place, we returned to the States occasionally to keep the flag raised in all we were doing. We now had eight churches with a total of 1,000 people attending, and six schools in six villages, bringing our total enrollment to 1,523 children. Besides our mission community house, church, and school in Bord Mer, George and I were finally able to move into our own three-room home, about the size of a two-car garage. But it was more than adequate for our needs. It had a large bare cement living room and two bedrooms. Although there was space for a kitchen, I had no appliances since I couldn't justify the $30 a month it would cost to keep a refrigerator and stove running, especially since we already had them at the community house.

It was wonderful to see some of the transformations that were taking place among the people. Not only was their appearance different, but many had now come to the Lord. And recently word had reached me that little Sherline, who hadn't been able to sit up as a 5-year-old and had been left to die, had been adopted by an American nurse and her husband. Already, since she was living in the States with her new family, she had several surgeries performed on her back. Soon we began receiving pictures of Sherline which we passed on to her family, giving them updated progress reports of her health as well.

It was also a real blessing to have our son, Charlie, working beside us, helping with city business and accounting work. He especially loved working with the local fishermen, supplying them with hooks, lines, and materials to repair and maintain their boats, and building strong relationships with them on a personal level.

A few weeks after celebrating our third anniversary in Haiti, I was in the city, visiting the Department of Education of U.S.A.I.D. They were being funded to help establish a school curriculum in Creole. Since everything was currently in French, I was anxious to get hold of some of their books for both our students and teachers.

Yet, as I walked into the agency, I couldn't help but notice how quiet it was—there was almost no one around. Suddenly, a woman worker stopped me. "What are you doing in the city?" she questioned.

"I have a whole list of business to do here."

"You better get right home. This country's about to undergo a political change at any moment. Don't come back until it's safe."

My pulse quickened as I tried to take in the unexpected news. If the woman was right, I knew I needed to get home. I had learned from my graduate studies that once a country experienced a political upheaval, chaos, instability, and danger quickly followed. Therefore, if Jean Claude Duvalier or "Baby Doc" was overthrown, I knew it would probably take years before things settled down.

Turning on my heels, I headed back to our mission, trying not to think about the tremendous consequences that a political revolt might have upon our beloved Haitian people.

Chapter 15

Uncertain Times

For the next month, the mission curtailed its business in the city and shopped locally. Then, on February 7, 1986, Duvalier fled the country peaceably and moved to France. Other supporters of Duvalier also fled the country. One was the Haitian man who owned land next to our mission and had smoothed our dirt road. Before he left, he sold his land to us for six thousand dollars. We hoped to eventually build a Mission Training Center there, complete with housing and dining facilities.

The personal police force of Duvalier was known as the Tonton Macoutes. Until now, they had controlled the people by intimidation and harsh punishments, wielding tremendous power over them. Many of the Tonton Macoutes had fled the country. Some remained behind, determined to try to control the new government.

Many of the voodoo priests were also members of the Tonton Macoutes and had enjoyed their power over the people. Now the Haitians had lost much of their fear and regard for the voodoo priests and had a greater sense of freedom.

Although the Tonton Macoutes had been cruel in their methods of keeping a tight control over the country, crime had been almost nonexistent. Yet, now that Duvalier had been overthrown, a smooth transition from a military government to a civilian one seemed impossible, especially since the Haitians knew little of the democratic process.

Chaos erupted. During one uprising, several children were shot and killed. Because of the increasing fear of student demonstrations, the new civilian government temporarily closed the schools.

There were other demonstrations as well, usually paid for by protesters of the current government. Each time, mobs of angry people carrying sticks and machetes ran through the streets of Port-au-Prince, shouting political slogans. I even heard that dismembered human heads were put on sticks and paraded through the streets, as well as pictures of other atrocities, to instill fear into the people.

Once word got out that a demonstration was to take place, shop owners clanged their metal gates shut and vehicles stayed off the road, afraid of spray paint and stones that might be directed at them. Fortunately, because the mobs eventually became hungry, the demonstrations were usually short-lived.

Roadblocks of burning tires or other obstacles were also set up on the highway in an effort to cripple the government. If you tried to pass, you might cause the wrath of those guarding the blockade, risking rocks or other forms of attack.

Despite the tremendous turmoil, we at NEW Missions had to ask ourselves: Were we going to allow our minds to become entangled with the political upheaval around us, or were we going to get on with what we were called to do— feeding, educating, and preaching the Gospel to the poor?

Certainly, we had plenty to keep us occupied. As a new mission, we were getting many young missionaries who required training. And since the school enrollment had jumped from 500 to 1,500 in one year, we were busy registering children, taking their photographs, cutting uniform material, and overseeing the facilities. In addition, I was doing most of the cooking and public relations work with

food and health agencies. While we were aware that the
political situation was volatile, we purposed to set our hearts
and minds to the task at hand. Despite the instability in Haiti
now, we still felt safe at our mission, which remained hidden
several miles from the highway and surrounded by villagers
who welcomed our presence.

During the past three years, I had pounded on the
doors of every international agency I knew, trying to get
help to drill a well. We still hadn't given up hope that someday we would have one. George had talked with another
well company, but to no avail. Even if they did find water,
they felt it would be full of salt since we were so close to the
ocean. However, after we persuaded an agency to drill a
half-mile away in Neply, which turned out to be successful,
they finally agreed to drill at our mission.

While George pointed to a spot at the back of our
property, an American southerner named Henry set up his
well-drilling equipment there. It was the furthest spot from
the ocean, yet a good location for allocating water to the rest
of the mission.

Several of us gathered at the site and prayed as Henry
took his rig and drilled down to 100 feet. The atmosphere
that day was as intense as the scorching heat that bore down
upon us.

"Henry," George asked, "what's down there?"

"There's mu-u-u-d down there," he responded in his
thick southern drawl.

George encouraged him to drill deeper. As we kept
praying, Henry continued to attach 20-foot sections of drill
pipe.

Finally, Henry got down to 160 feet. "What do you
see?" George asked again.

"There's rock down there!"

George brightened noticeably as my heart gave a little
leap: We all knew that rock was a good sign.

After Henry bore down to 180 feet, he let out a holler: "There's water down there! There's a *lot* of water down there!"

I could hardly contain my elation as water spouted up out of the shaft. Henry quickly began disconnecting his pipe and stacking it on top of his 30-ton truck, afraid it might sink into the mud and never get out. He drove his rig away from the area as fast as he could.

We pounded casing down into the bottom of the well, and water gushed up four feet out of it, flooding the entire area. It turned out we had struck an aquifer—a lake under pressure—which meant that we didn't even need a pump or tank. As water flowed through our 10-acre compound in incredible abundance, I felt as though we had just entered the Promised Land. But instead of flowing with milk and honey, we were flowing with water!

The water wasn't full of salt as predicted. Later we learned that the salt water theory was inaccurate. Pressure comes not from the ocean inland but from the land out to the sea.

We capped the well with a big cement base to hold the casing in place and put in a valve to control the flow of water. As the Haitians gathered and looked, they were amazed by our demonstration of how the water could be turned on and off through the valve.

It wasn't long before agencies and other missions found out about our well. Soon a UNICEF engineer was dispatched. After questioning us, he went down the coast and had a well dug down to 180 feet. Immediately he found water, and everyone there thought he was a genius.

Meanwhile, our mission continued to thrive as we concentrated our energies on the tasks at hand. Unfortunately we were losing our son, Charlie, who decided to return to Worcester and begin college. What an asset he had been to us in Haiti for the past three years.

Despite the political upheaval, I felt it was time to focus my efforts on starting a women's ministry. As I began planning, memories of my wonderful experiences with Women's Aglow came flooding back, challenging me to forge ahead. Not only did I want to bless and encourage these Haitian women, but I prayed that it would further strengthen my relationship with them as well, especially in these dark, uncertain times.

Chapter 16

Reaching Out to the Haitian Women

Two dozen women, wearing their nicest dresses, sat on wooden chairs in one of our school classrooms, giddy and talkative. Although class started at 9:00 A.M. it was 9:30 A.M. by the time they had finally arrived from Bord Mer and Neply—no one ever seemed concerned about keeping a schedule. Several toddlers roamed the room. Even Rosette's little year-old Judy, whose cord had been wrapped around her neck at birth, was there.

I asked each woman her name and how many children she had. I passed out paper and colored magic markers. Then, hoping to make them more conscious of who they were as women, I explained that they were to draw a picture of themselves.

The women smiled shyly, then picked up their markers awkwardly, having never held one before.

"Rosette," I asked as Judy played at her feet, "do you have a face?"

She giggled nervously, and I walked over and helped her draw one.

"Apie," I said to an elderly grandmother, "do you have one ear?" As she laughed along with the other women, I smiled and answered for her: "Oh, you have two ears."

Soon Apie had drawn a face, two ears, and little curls around her head, making her hair as pretty as possible.

I had the women draw their bodies, telling them to make two circles for their breasts. I knew that breasts were very important to them and represented nourishment for their babies. And often, even if a woman had no milk, she would still let her hungry baby suck to keep him or her quiet.

After they finished their drawings, I explained that God had made each one of them unique; I hoped that they would see themselves as distinct and loved individuals, not merely as the property of a man. I wanted them to think of themselves in terms of a woman, accepted and created by God. Then after I wrote their names on their papers and collected them, I explained that I would take the papers home as a way to remember to pray for them.

The next week I used their drawings to further illustrate their uniqueness. Eventually I took photographs of all the women and wrote their names on them so I could greet them personally.

Before each class, I tried to interact with the women as much as possible while they munched on something sweet—usually a cookie or brownie. I also made sure we had enough goodies so that we didn't have hungry children in our classroom. Besides, whenever I had a women's meeting in the States, we always had plenty of food available, even though most of the women weren't that hungry—nor did they necessarily need it.

Soon another missionary named Mary Jane—a healthy-looking, blonde, blue-eyed nurse—worked alongside me in the women's ministry. Eventually she branched out into other villages, training and teaching the women there. As the women's ministry continued to grow, I tried to make the meetings as special as I could, bringing little gifts whenever possible.

One morning I was approached by a Haitian woman who complained that I hadn't had a meeting in their village for a long time and that they needed encouragement.

I suddenly felt annoyed. *Why did these Haitians always want something?* I questioned inwardly. *When would they stop begging?*

But then I stopped myself. These were women who didn't even have the money to eat every day. These were women I was called to serve and to give myself to whole-heartedly. Besides, wasn't I the one who was always asking God to use me?

I knew that God was a giver, and as long as I had an attitude of generosity, He would put something in my hands to give. And, if I did go, 60 Haitian women would have the opportunity to hear about Jesus.

Then I remembered some lace and five dozen face cloths I had recently purchased. "You tell the women I'm coming," I replied, "—and tell them I'm going to bring them something nice."

After sewing ruffled lace on each of the face cloths, I passed them out to the women of that village. Several weeks later, at a church service, I watched these same women wearing their fancy lace face cloths on top of their heads.

One simple face cloth and a piece of lace had brightened their lives so much—and it had been such an easy thing for me to do.

One Sunday morning during our church service, I saw a Haitian woman demonstrate giving in a different kind of way—one that humbled me. In the congregation were two babies—Adelina and Jonathan—born just one month apart to one father and two mothers who lived just five huts from each other. While the one mother nursed Adelina, she heard Jonathan, who was with his grandmother, wailing loudly, six rows behind her. Since Jonathan's mother was absent, the other mother turned around and reached out her arms towards him. Quickly, the baby was handed from one Haitian to the next until the mother took Jonathan in her arms, nursing him until he quieted down.

My heart melted. If I were in that situation, would I have been capable of nursing the baby of my man's other woman? Slowly I was learning that these women had tremendous tolerance and forgiveness in order to help one another survive—something that I as an American woman wasn't sure I could ever do.

Although many women were attending our meetings and extending love and forgiveness towards one another, some of them still had a hard time letting go of their voodoo superstitions. One of them was an older pregnant woman who had gone into labor and was now having difficulties delivering her baby.

Accompanied by a nurse and another missionary, I entered her mud hut and was immediately uncomfortable. Several old women hovered over the pregnant woman, performing voodoo. One of the women had a conch shell, attached to a string, which they ran over her belly while they chanted incessantly.

Trying to keep my emotions in control, I explained to the pregnant woman, "This is your baby and your house. I will stay, sing and encourage you, and the nurse will help you with your delivery. But you'll have to choose whether to have the presence of God in your home or to have voodoo. We won't stay if you want to have both."

Hesitantly, the pregnant woman told the others to leave, and they did so peaceably. But I could tell it was difficult for her, especially since some of them were relatives.

For the next several hours we sang songs and read the Bible as the woman's labor became more and more intense. Finally, after a difficult breech birth, a baby boy was born.

iIn the past, I avoided voodoo whenever possible, confronting it only when necessary. We knew that we were children of God; therefore, greater was He that was in us than he that was in the world. Even the new Haitian Christians called God the *Gran Met*—the big Master. As a result, they no longer feared the voodoo priests because they knew we were in touch with a much greater power.

Once, however, I walked past a voodoo temple that was open. A voodoo priest was inside with several women I recognized. In his hands, the priest held a chicken by its wings as it fought to get away. Quickly he broke the wings of the chicken, then took its head and twisted it until it became detached. Then, after letting the body fall to the ground, he threw the head of the chicken towards the women as blood splattered all over them. As I turned away with a heavy heart, the verse from Hebrews 10:10 flashed through my mind: "...we have been made holy through the sacrifice of the body of Jesus Christ once for all." How I prayed for opportunities to teach them from God's Word, especially about Jesus, who already gave Himself as a sacrificial lamb for each one of us.

Another time, one of our 8-year-old school boys came to our clinic with his leg swollen and infected. Later, after we got him on antibiotics, one of the voodoo priest's nephews remarked, "I bet he walked on voodoo magic powder that was meant to kill somebody else."

My ears perked up. "What kind of powder are you talking about?"

"They grind bones of dead animals with other potions that are poisonous. Then they spread them in the pathway of people whom they want to die."

I turned away, disturbed at the control by fear that voodoo had on these people. Not only that, but I knew it was making them financially poorer. One anthropologist who lived in Haiti for 10 years discovered that when the Haitians sold their land, 75 percent of the time they did so to pay for a voodoo ritual. Whenever a voodoo priest says an angry spirit is causing a Haitian's sickness or calamity, he charges them for the ritual he'll perform to appease the spirit. As a result, many Haitians feel they have no alternative but to sell their land.

Voodoo left its mark in other ways as well. Yolene was a young teenage girl who lived in Birey. I often saw her stripped naked, pulling at her long, braided hair and beating at her body, completely out of her mind. Many times she threw herself into the water to drown, but her relatives always managed to intervene.

Eventually one of our nurses brought her to our clinic to see if she had epilepsy, but she was fine. Instead, she let them know that she was serving Satan.

When I saw Yolene in her tormented state, I admonished her and her family to come to Jesus. Yet each time, her face would twist in a defiant expression as she hurled insults at me.

After a year and a half, Yolene came to me and said she was a Christian. I remained somewhat skeptical, especially since she refused to acknowledge that she no longer served Satan. Now that she was in our school program, I could only pray that we might influence her relationship with God even further.

Meanwhile, as I busied myself with the women's ministry, George was busy as well. One day, he and Timothy took the boat out, stopping at a small fishing village called Ti Riviere. The place was full of children, but there was no school or church in the village. Soon afterwards, George met a woman missionary in Port-au-Prince who had tried for seven years to get a church or school going somewhere in Haiti. She agreed to return to the States to raise money for a school for the children of Ti Riviere and to try and find sponsors for them. We gave her photographs of 57 children from the village. We went ahead and built a cement school for the children, trusting that we would soon see some money coming in from the woman's efforts.

That fall we returned to the States for one month to share with different churches about our mission's progress. Besides the 1,500 students who were now in our schools, we hoped to eventually be able to accommodate even more children.

It was also good to be home with George, Jr. and Charlie. George, Jr. was doing a fine job of running our mission office while Charlie attended a local college. Mary Ann had just graduated from college and was now living in Miami, doing graduate studies. Timothy decided to remain behind in Worcester to attend his first year of high school. Fortunately, Charlie planned on returning with us to Haiti for a few months. Not only did he miss the people, but since our mission was growing so fast, we desperately needed him.

After two weeks at home, I saw a doctor for my annual checkup. After the physical examination, my doctor grew grave. "You have a lump in your left breast," he explained. "We must schedule a biopsy immediately."

Chapter 17

Jehovah Jireh

I sat in shock. Those were words that other women heard—not me.

I returned home, my emotions numb as I broke the news to George. As I sank into his arms, he hugged me tightly and, for the first time, I let myself cry.

The next day one of the best radiologists in the area sat me down. "It doesn't look good," she explained. "Not only do you have a lump on your left breast, but there looks like a lot of fibroid tissue on your right one. Be prepared for a mastectomy."

My life passed before me like a video spinning on fast-forward. The cold, awful truth was facing me head-on, and I didn't want to accept it. I was so fulfilled in the work George and I had started three and a half years ago in Haiti. Yet now my very future was being threatened.

Dr. Clermont, an excellent Christian surgeon, scheduled a biopsy in a few days. As I waited, I wavered between trusting God and experiencing moments of sheer panic.

I certainly had lots of prayer on my behalf. Soon word reached me that the Haitian women were praying and fasting for me, trusting that God would return me to them in complete health.

After my biopsy was performed, Dr. Clermont visited me. Although he wouldn't know the results for a couple of days, he said that he was now very hopeful. Meanwhile, I was able to share with him stories of our work in Haiti. When I told him of the plight of the children there, he was deeply moved, having already adopted 10 needy children from around the world. He also decided to perform my surgery as a gift since I didn't have medical insurance at the time.

Two days later, he asked me to meet him at his office. Twisting my fingers together in my lap, I sat pensively in the waiting room. Finally, Dr. Clermont ushered me into his office.

Smiling broadly, he explained, "There's no cancer at all."

A flood of relief washed over me as I silently thanked the Lord. One week later, George, Charlie, and I returned to Haiti, right on schedule.

∾ ∾ ∾ ∾ ∾

A few weeks later, while passing through Neply, I noticed a little naked girl about 6 years old with her arms and legs tied together. Foaming at the mouth and unable to move, she was sitting alone in the dirt—crying, hot, and miserable.

Soon I discovered that her name was Edna, and she came from a very large and poor family. Her mother, Olimcia—an older woman of medium height with a tight, nervous face—had already suffered tremendous heartache. Her first husband had died, leaving her with four children, and pregnant with Edna. She had another man now, but six babies had died because the mother's milk was not agreeable to the babies. Once, she brought her newborn baby to us, but we had just run out of formula. One of our nurses tried a substitute, but the baby developed diarrhea and died.

Now, unable to deal with her daughter's seizures, Olimcia had simply tied Edna up so she wouldn't stand and hurt herself. I knew it wasn't just the physical suffering that was so hard on her daughter. In Haiti, the handicapped are often taunted and ridiculed, and called a *kokobe*, a Creole word for "baby coconut," but referring in this context to a person who is mentally lacking or handicapped.

I brought Edna to the clinic where we discovered that she had epilepsy. Immediately she was placed on phenobarbitol, which was able to control and finally stop her seizures altogether. But because her right side had been weakened by her previous seizures, she dragged her right foot as she walked; also, her right hand did not hang normally.

An American visitor met Edna and wanted to sponsor her; soon she began attending kindergarten. How precious she looked in her yellow gingham uniform. Every Sunday morning she attended our women's ministry class with her mother, Olimcia. Each time I saw Edna, she beamed brightly at me and gave me hugs, letting me know how grateful she was to be walking again.

While I continued to monitor Edna's progress, the mission was also progressing as well. Despite the fact that the country was still in political chaos, we were expanding rapidly, now searching for land for a high school and Bible school.

In the meantime, I was making my home more comfortable, realizing that we planned to be here for a long time. With George and Kelli's encouragement, I bought a couch, dresser, hutch, and glass-top table, all made of bamboo. Then my parents bought us lovely imitation marble tile for the floor. Eventually we even decided to add a refrigerator and stove, which were especially convenient for the increasing number of visitors we had.

Shortly afterwards, I received word that my daughter had been in a car accident in Miami. Although George, Jr. had flown from Worcester to be with her, and she appeared to be okay, I was filled with worry, especially since I had received the news several days after the fact. How could I trust God to take care of my children when I was so far away, helpless to do anything for them? How could anyone take the place of a mother? Over and over I cried out to God, asking Him to be a mother to my children in my absence. As much as I loved my missionary calling, I sometimes found it difficult to fully surrender my children into God's hands, trusting Him to watch over them while I was away.

On May 11, after taking Charlie to the airport to return to college, we made a long-anticipated purchase—our first air-conditioned passenger vehicle, a sparkling tan Pajero. Finally, we could roll up our windows and lock them, helping us to not only avoid further thievery but enabling us to pass through roadblocks of fire when necessary.

Three days later, I packed cheese, grape juice, and linen napkins, anticipating our first day off in six months. George and I planned to drive three hours south to Cayes, a place we had always wanted to visit.

I looked at my watch. It was already 8:30 A.M. and we should have been gone. However, I also knew that if anything happened at the school, clinic, or construction site, I could expect to wait even longer.

As 9:00 A.M. rolled around, I could feel my frustration mounting. Silently I prayed, *Oh God, I don't want to be mad. But George promised me this day off.*

Finally, at 9:30 A.M., George appeared, and we took off immediately, glad to finally escape for the day. Even though I was fulfilled in what we were doing, it was wonderful to have some time for just the two of us—away from the constant stream of people.

After an hour, George decided to pull over at a food stand to buy a cold soda. Just as we came to a stop, a crowded vehicle full of Americans pulled up alongside of us.

"Where are you going?" the young blonde-haired driver asked.

"To Cayes."

The driver explained that he was working with a Haitian pastor in the area and was taking a group of visitors to Cayes for the day. "Would you be willing to take a couple of our people with you?"

Inwardly I groaned. How was I supposed to respond when it was my one day off in six months and I had already left two hours later than I wanted? Now, just one hour into my trip, when I was finally enjoying some precious time alone with my husband, some Americans ask us for a ride in our brand-new car.

"Sure, hop in," George said before I could respond.

Although I silently protested, I realized that living in the church for three years had still been a good training ground. George and I both had learned that interruptions were simply part of being in the ministry.

Two men climbed into the back of our vehicle, and soon we became acquainted. Jim—a slender 40-year-old of medium height—was a real-estate agent, and Harry—a few years older—was a jolly, peace-loving pastor who started Creation Festivals in Pennsylvania, which featured top Christian entertainers and speakers. Soon we were sharing our cheese and grape juice with them.

As we chatted with the two men, George and I tried to be very careful about what we said about our mission. We often heard of visitors who came to see a particular mission in Haiti, only to be lured away by other missionaries to support their work instead. As a result, we wanted to make sure we remained ethical.

After arriving in Cayes, we all had lunch together. Afterwards, the driver approached us: "I really don't have much for these people to do. Do you mind if we visit your mission this weekend? Can we come for dinner Saturday night?"

Once again I felt a bit put out. Saturday was a day off for all of our missionaries, and I wasn't too excited about making dinner for 15 people all by myself. I was already doing most of the mission cooking and preparing meals every Sunday afternoon as well.

George agreed again, and for the rest of the afternoon I tried to push the whole unpleasant affair to the back of my mind. Instead, I focused my attention on the last few hours George and I had together before returning home to our mission.

Two days later, on the Saturday my guests were to arrive, I was busy making bread and spaghetti sauce when a Haitian woman approached me. She explained that a woman had just delivered a baby a few villages away and needed someone to cut the cord.

My shoulders slumped as I drew a deep breath. *Lord, I prayed silently. I have no nurses. I'm all alone and I'm having company. Should I go?*

I knew the answer. Would I choose to be selfish just because I was busy and tired?

Peeling off my apron, I hastened to the clinic. After finding what I needed, I asked a teenage girl to accompany me since she often assisted the nurses in the past. Then we jumped into our pickup truck and sped off to the village.

A short time later, I cut the cord of a baby girl and was given the honor of naming her. I named her Sheryl, after a pastor's wife I would be seeing soon in Miami. I returned to our mission in plenty of time to finish my dinner preparations.

After the Americans arrived and we had dinner together, George told Jim and Harry about our school in Ti Riviere. He explained that a woman missionary had promised to find sponsors for the children in that village. Yet now, after an entire year of feeding and educating the children ourselves, we still did not have one child sponsored.

"How many children are there?" Jim inquired.

"Fifty-seven," George replied.

"Fifty-seven children." Jim paused. "That explains why I'm here." He then went on to share that a year ago, he asked for God's direction in his life and he felt Him say, *Go to Haiti—Fifty-seven children.*

Jim's face broke out into a warm smile. "I didn't know what God meant until now… I'm going to sponsor all fifty-seven of those children."

My heart did a little somersault, hardly believing what I had just heard. As the realization grew, I felt overjoyed that these children would all be sponsored. But along with my happiness, I was also greatly humbled by the important lesson I had learned. Although our first meeting with Jim on the way to Cayes now certainly seemed like a divine appointment, I almost ruined it because of my own agenda. Had we left at a different time or had I insisted on my own private time with George, we would have missed out on God's greater plan for that day. As a result, I realized that unless I was willing to remain flexible, God would be hindered in His ability to use me.

∞ ∞ ∞ ∞ ∞

Jim returned to his church of 10,000 members in California, and eventually others took over in sponsoring some of the 57 children. Later, as our enrollment in Ti Riviere grew to 250 children, the church members sponsored each of the new students as well. Meanwhile, Jim continued to visit several times a year, also bringing church groups with him, as well as his Missions Director and pastor, Tim Timmons.

Pastor Harry became an ongoing blessing, too, sponsoring children in other villages as well and returning several times, both alone and with a group. Whenever he came, he spent most of his time meandering through the village of Neply, visiting as many people as possible.

On May 21, just a week after Jim and Harry left, we were able to purchase seven acres of land on the main highway, just one mile from the center of Leogane. Eventually we planned to build a high school there which would accommodate 1,000 students.

Then, amidst the whirl of activity at our mission, my back went out of place. Barely able to walk, I spent my days lying on a sheet near the entrance of our home, where I was close to the kitchen and bathroom and accessible to anyone who needed me. Yet, as I found some relief on the cold, hard tile, as well as an escape from the soaring summer temperatures, my mind buzzed with all the things I wanted to do. I had always experienced such wonderful health, yet now I found myself helpless to do anything.

The political situation had remained shaky ever since Duvalier had fled the country a year and a half earlier. Demonstrations continued four days a week, and gas stations had now been ordered to remain closed indefinitely in an attempt to stop the constant roadblocks of fire.

After two weeks, my back finally healed, yet I noticed that my body felt strangely weak. But I was sure that once I got moving and back into my job responsibilities, I would soon feel back to normal.

One morning as I pulled myself from sleep, I gazed through my sliding-glass door into our backyard. Suddenly a chill shot up my spine as my body stiffened: A red cloth had been tied to our barbed wire, a sign that voodoo was being performed on George or me.

I felt physically shaken. After regaining my composure, I immediately had one of our workers remove it. Later, I found out that a red cloth is used in performing voodoo when a person wants something and is trying to elicit good favor.

During the next few days, however, I felt more like I was being cursed. It was becoming more and more difficult for me to breathe, and I was experiencing a sharp pain in my rib cage. Soon I became so weak that I could barely walk from my house to the mission community house 75 feet away, where we ate our meals.

Two days later, on a sweltering, humid afternoon, I lay on my sofa, trying to rest. Then, through the haze of interrupted sleep, I saw a light-colored casket, made out of silver metallic steel. Slowly, silently, the casket slid open on its hinge. As I gazed at the person inside, my eyes widened in horror: It was me!

The casket clanged shut, and I saw a figure hovering in the background with silvery-metallic skin, a pointed head, misshapen ears, and ugly greenish-yellow eyes. His evil laughter echoed through my room as he rejoiced over the fact that I was dead.

Slowly, methodically, the casket opened and shut as the air thickened all around me and I fought to breathe.

After several minutes, the image disappeared and left me shaking and fearful. Forcing my thoughts heavenward, I tried to remind myself that God's desires for me were always for healing and life.

While I kept this horrible experience quiet, three of our nurses continued to check on me, baffled over my weakening condition. Even their prayers seemed to be blocked, as though they were falling on deaf ears.

No one seemed to understand why I wasn't getting better. Was I under some demonic attack because the women's ministry was growing and so many were getting saved and leaving voodoo?

I didn't know the answers. I just knew I had to get well.

Chapter 18

Setback

The weeks turned into a month. By July, I was still declining physically, becoming even weaker. Today, however, my spirits were buoyed. Timothy had returned to Haiti after spending the last nine months attending high school in Worcester. Unfortunately, on the way to our mission, George and Timothy had run into an unexpected demonstration. Met by angry mobs, George had bulldozed through a dozen roadblocks of fire at high speeds, realizing it was impossible to negotiate with any of the demonstrators.

Now that they arrived safely at our mission, Timothy would remain here and continue his studies through correspondence. He also planned to start up a band and several music groups to participate in our church services and revival meetings.

One week after Timothy's arrival, Kelli became increasingly alarmed over my condition, telling George to get me to the States immediately. Since I already had an open-ended return trip ticket—a requirement for non-Haitian residents—I was ready to go. Since the political situation in Haiti was becoming increasingly desperate, George would have to remain behind. A general strike had been in effect since June, crippling the country even further. Travel had also become more dangerous, making it even more difficult for our missionaries to purchase necessary supplies in the city and to meet people at the airport. And now, along with the economic conditions, violence continued to erupt throughout the country. More and more, individuals were being subjected to *dechouke* a term the Haitians shouted during their demonstrations, which meant to tear somebody down and destroy all they had—their home, vehicle, land, and often their lives. Therefore, as much as I wanted my husband beside me, I knew that George was needed more than ever right where he was.

The day of my departure was Wednesday, a day when there wasn't supposed to be any demonstrations. George practically carried me to our car. When he started the engine, it became obvious that we were almost out of gas: The needle remained on empty, refusing to budge even a little.

Somehow we managed to make it to the outskirts of Port-au-Prince before we finally ran out of fuel. Since all the gas stations were closed and the only way we could buy gas was on the black market, George explained, "I'll put you in a Haitian taxi that will take you to the airport. As soon as I get gas, I'll come and find you."

George flagged down a small beat-up taxi, and I was placed next to the driver on a seat that was completely torn apart. Holding my side as we bounced along, I could actually see the road beneath me as we traveled. I felt sick and afraid, and tears spilled from my eyes, drying rapidly from the suffocating heat.

When we miraculously arrived at the airport 20 minutes later, my heart sank: The ticket line extended all the way to the end of the room. Feeling too weak to stand, I scanned the line for an American to help me. While I looked, my breathing suddenly became more and more labored. There was air all around me but I couldn't breathe. Engulfed in a sea of faces, I sank to the floor and lay on my side in order to catch my breath.

As I fought to get enough air, several faces stared at me, then turned away, unwilling to help. A few minutes later, the face of an Oriental woman appeared, hovering over me: "What can I do to help you?"

"I'm sick. Here's my ticket and passport," I whispered, shoving them at her. "Get me on this plane."

The woman nodded, then left as I struggled to sit up.

A few minutes later, the Oriental woman reappeared. After returning my ticket and passport to me, she explained, "You now have a seat on the next plane leaving for Miami."

After I thanked her and the woman left, I realized she must have had some sort of connections to get me on so quickly. Regardless of how she did it, I was grateful that there was one Good Samaritan in the crowd. Later, I discovered how fortunate it was that no American Airlines agent realized I was sick.

After saying goodbye to George, who arrived minutes before my departure, I boarded the plane and slept fitfully on the flight to Miami. Once we landed, I called George, Jr. to meet me in Boston. Although I was still terribly sick, I was relieved to be back in the States where I could receive excellent medical care.

George, Jr. and Charlie met me at the Boston airport and brought me to our Victorian home, which also doubled as our mission office. I was glad to be back in familiar surroundings, especially since sharp pains were jolting through my lungs and my hands felt tingly all over. It was almost as though my body was spinning out of control and I was unable to stop it.

After I swallowed several aspirin, the pain in my lungs seemed to subside a little. Heading for my bedroom a few minutes later, I told my sons I would see a doctor in the morning.

At 4:00 A.M., I jolted from sleep as piercing pain shot through my right side. Struggling to breathe, I crawled into George, Jr.'s bedroom and woke him. "Get me to the hospital right now," I rasped out in a dry whisper.

"What's wrong?" George, Jr. asked, his voice full of alarm.

"I can barely breathe. The pain is so bad."

Within minutes, George, Jr. rushed me into the emergency room at the University of Massachusetts Hospital. After a nurse took my blood pressure, the room became electric with activity. Immediately I was hooked up to an IV as a physician and several nurses huddled around me, injecting me in my arms and legs with high doses of antibiotics and morphine.

During the next several hours my parents, sons and friends visited. Time passed for me in a nightmarish fog. Drugged and delirious, I actually thought my bed was a deep, narrow, wooden Haitian boat that was sinking in dark, murky waters. Each time I became conscious, my body felt racked with pain, and I actually felt that my mattress was trying to kill me. Once, when I became aware of my family weeping beside me, I whispered, "Just pray. I guess there's a battle going on for my life."

After a long, tense 18 hours, I was finally stable enough to be admitted to a private room. Yet, when the doctors and nurses found out I had been living in Haiti, no one dared enter my room without a mask, gloves, and gown on. Suddenly, I became this woman who was probably full of all sorts of diseases. Since I was at a teaching hospital, groups of medical students and interns visited me periodically, draped in masks and gowns. Each time they came, unreasonable fear gripped me as I felt convinced that they were all evil agents out to destroy me. Over and over again, I cried out for Jesus to deliver me, and to fill me with strength and hope once again. Only then did I feel new life breathed into me and the courage to keep fighting.

After I had been in the hospital two days, one of the nurses, who took care of me earlier walked into my room. Seeing me, surprise registered on her face. "Oh, you made it."

I nodded weakly.

After the nurse finished puttering about my bedside, adjusting IV drips and monitoring my vital signs, a doctor entered the room. He informed me that I had double pneumonia—meaning I had fluid in both lungs—probably as a result of lying on my back on the cold, damp tile floor for two weeks.

Meanwhile, the medical team who visited me were always coming up with a different diagnosis, wanting to take more and more tests. Despite the seriousness of my condition, I became very concerned that I had no medical insurance. Although we were still renting our three-family apartment house, the money was all going to help put our children through college.

After five days in the hospital, I asked the doctor when I could go home.

Immediately he shook his head. "That's not something we can even talk about yet."

Later that day, I asked the radiologist, who was on our mission's Board of Directors, the same question. Gently, she explained that they didn't know the condition of my lungs yet; there were also some suspicious-looking growths on them.

Still worried about the enormous hospital bill I was incurring, I asked my nurse if I could talk with someone who took care of the patient billing.

Soon a middle-aged woman appeared in my room. After hearing my situation, the woman looked grim. Without a word, she turned on her heels and left.

Two hours later, my doctor appeared. After he gave me a prescription for oral medication and directions on how to chart my temperature, my parents appeared. Then, after a nurse pulled my IV, I was informed that I was discharged from the hospital.

Panic gripped me like a vice as I shot a questioning look at my parents. With eyes full of concern, my parents tried to gently ease me from my bed. But my arms and legs felt heavy, and I didn't think I could move. When they finally did manage to help me stand, I felt the blood rush from my face and my legs go weak from shock. With great difficulty, Mom and Dad half-carried me out to their car, and finally managed to get me to their home where they could take care of me.

The first night in my parents' home, I stumbled into their bedroom, waking them from sleep. Stifling a sob, I struggled to form a word, to make my throat push out a sound. "I'm afraid I'm...going to die. Can I sleep with you?"

Mom and Dad nodded reassuringly, trying to mask the concern I knew they were feeling. As I slipped in next to Mom and curled into a fetal position, my fear eased a little, just knowing they were there. And when they finally drifted back to sleep, I stayed awake, thinking of how supportive they were of George and me throughout the years. Now, at 45 years of age, I realized I needed them more than ever.

The next few days passed in a blur as my temperature became completely erratic, switching from one degree below or one degree above normal. Able to eat only sparingly and completely devoid of energy, I found myself sinking deeper and deeper into melancholy.

One night sleep eluded me as thoughts I had pushed down stirred and began to surface. Unreasonable fear gripped me as questions echoed and repeated in my mind: *What if I got this sick again in Haiti? Maybe next time I wouldn't be so lucky. Maybe next time it would be too late.*

Rolling on my side, I curled up into a ball and tried not to think about it. But I was unable to fall asleep, plagued by waves of doubt. Finally, I pulled out my Bible and turned to the book of Psalms. Immediately a verse from Psalm 17:8

jumped out at me: "Hide me in the shadow of Thy wings." As I pictured myself secure and nestled in the shadow of His wings, holding onto Him as my hope and refuge, my fears slowly subsided as I drifted off into a deep sleep.

I saw a few people over the next couple of weeks, but I tried to keep as low a profile as possible. A part of me was somewhat afraid of returning to Haiti, but a much bigger part of me was plagued by guilt: We had a mission in Haiti. We had hungry children in Haiti. We had work that needed to be done if the Haitians were to flourish. But now the missionary was sick. Useless. A person who had abandoned her post.

Therefore, I decided it was better that people didn't know what I was going through. Instead, just like I felt during my childhood when I heard the story of my birth, I wanted to hide.

After I had been home from the hospital for a month, George was finally able to spend a week with me. He explained that all our friends in Haiti were praying for me and for my speedy return. As uncomfortable as I knew George was around sickness, it was nevertheless wonderful to have him with me. And as I felt his love and reassurance, my spirits brightened considerably.

After George left, I spoke with Dr. Clermont, the doctor who operated on me when I was told I probably had breast cancer. "You'll know you're all better," he explained, "when you can stay awake all day and feel strong enough to want to do something. Don't go back to Haiti until then."

I had moved back into my own house with George, Jr. and Charlie, cooking for them whenever I felt well enough. Meanwhile, my husband kept me abreast of the progress at our mission where ten churches and seven schools were now flourishing. Construction was also still under way for our new training center next to our original property. This would give us additional housing for missionaries and visiting teams as well as a new dining facility. Soon it would be completed.

In August, a new Haitian constitution called for national elections to take place on November 29. No election had taken place since 1957, when Francois Duvalier was elected president of Haiti. Although this was good news, the atmosphere remained tense, and the economic conditions grew even worse because of the political uncertainty in the country. Now people were flooding the already overcrowded city of Port-au-Prince, desperately looking for something to sustain them. Many Haitians tried to flee to other countries, but strict immigration laws limited the number of people who could obtain entry visas. Some Haitians had resorted to leaving on small wooden boats for other islands in the Caribbean. Unfortunately, since the boats were dangerously overloaded, many persons perished before arriving at their destinations.

George often likened Haiti's economic circumstances to that of a large leaky boat in the middle of the ocean. Since the boat had a hole in the bottom, it was listing on its side, ready to go under. Inside the boat, people were frantically bailing out the water with buckets. Yet, no matter how hard they worked, more water was rushing in through the hole than was being bailed out.

Two problems facing Haiti were the deterioration of its natural resources and its increasing population. Fifty years ago, these two factors met and crossed each other, pushing Haiti over the brink of disaster. Once a paradise, it had now turned into a wasteland as people were robbed of their creativity and vitality; their dignity brought low by inhumane conditions.

Could the natural resources of Haiti ever be restored again, and could its mushrooming population ever be brought under control? Personally, George and I felt that the leaky hole could be plugged if the people would turn to God, allowing Him to raise up men and women equal to the task. For God, our Great Deliverer and Redeemer, was the only one who could deliver the Haitians from their plight. Often through history, we realized that when things appeared the darkest, God moved afresh by His Spirit to bring men and women to faith and to change the moral and social structures of societies. How we prayed that they might turn to Him in their time of need.

Despite the mounting chaos in the country, George and I saw the Haitians' future far from gloomy, holding onto the promise in Romans 5:5, which tells us that those who hope in God will not be disappointed. As a result, we were still full of vision for the good things God wanted for them. And now, after two months of recuperation—feeling almost back to my old self again—I finally flew out of Boston with a new expectancy in my heart as I returned to the people I had grown to love. Now, more than ever before, I prayed that God would use all of us at NEW Missions to help train a "New Generation" of Haitians who would bring about the change their country so desperately needed.

Chapter 19

Out of the Frying Pan, Into the Fire

I had been back in Haiti for only six weeks when George and I were on our way to Port-au-Prince to take Timothy to the airport. From there, he'd take a plane back to the States to attend a wedding. Unexpectedly, we were stopped by a demonstration. Peering out of our dust-caked window, I felt my heart beat double-time as I realized our vehicle was surrounded by men with angry faces and clenched teeth. Soon they were jostling our vehicle from side to side. George wasted no time in stepping on the accelerator, speeding us away from them.

Just a half-mile down the highway, we were stopped by a roadblock of burning tires and car wreckage. Two young Haitian men approached us, their eyes ablaze with anger. Since I knew that being on the road would be viewed as an unsupportive action against their political beliefs, I rolled down my window a crack and explained, "We're so sorry about what's happening to your country—and that we're on the road."

The men stared at me with a furious silence. Then I noticed the pile of rocks next to them. I knew of other missionaries who were caught at roadblocks and whose vehicles had been confiscated. It was also difficult not to think about the atrocities that were taking place within the country. My cheeks felt hot and red as I tried to slow my breathing. "We're praying things will change," I explained, trying to reason with them. "Please—we need to get to the airport."

It was obvious to George that these men were in no mood to negotiate. Flashing them a look of defiant determination, he blared his horn and gunned the engine. Then we raced through the fire as I held my breath until we were through. After George drove us halfway to the city where he saw several more roadblocks in the distance, he turned around and headed back to our mission, where we arrived safely a short time later. Timothy never did make it to the wedding.

∞ ∞ ∞ ∞ ∞

A few months later, I got pneumonia again. Immediately I got the same medication I took before I had returned to Haiti, enabling me to recover in three weeks.

On November 29, the day set aside for presidential elections, the military government prevented the elections from taking place. We knew this would only lead to further civil unrest, and that the country would not begin to make progress until a democratically-elected civilian government was in place. As things stood now, every six months a new president was in office. Each time a new one took over, the president's first concern was to stay alive. To make himself as secure as possible, he immediately installed his friends in all key government positions. However, by the time the new president's programs were finally adopted and approved, he was overthrown and another president was put in office, with new people and new ideas. Therefore, nothing was ever accomplished.

Since Duvalier left the country, there had been an increase of robberies in Haiti, especially in Port-au-Prince. The Tonton Macoutes—the private police of Duvalier— were blamed for many of them. Guns remained in their hands while the new government worked toward having them arrested or killed.

Although we were removed from the political and civil strife going on in the country, we began experiencing small robberies, at least once a month. Occasionally, when missionaries returned to their rooms, their sheets or bedding would be missing. The robbers also broke into our kitchen, taking meat and eggs, as well as a blender that George, Jr. had recently sent to us.

We assumed that the robbers were not from our village because our people were benefiting too greatly from our mission; therefore, they would not want us to become angry with them and leave. Also, it is a great shame for a Haitian to be caught stealing; if he is, he carries the name "thief" the rest of his life, and his children are known as the "children of a thief." It was possible, though, that someone in our village had made a business deal with someone coming by boat from one of the islands across the bay; there were also people who lived in our village from some of those islands. By boat, stolen goods could be carried away quickly from the scene of the crime.

Soon an incident occurred which brought the seriousness of the situation to the forefront.

It was springtime, so I decided to do something special for 40 of my most faithful women involved in our women's ministry. I planned a weekend retreat for us at a Baptist mission in the mountains, about three hours away. On the morning of the retreat I bounded out of bed, eager to leave. Peering out my window, I could see that most of the women had already gathered, even though we weren't leaving for another hour and a half. Smiling, I knew our time together would be special and meaningful.

Just then, George appeared in the doorway, disappointment clouding his face. "A terrible thing has happened," he explained tersely. "There's been a robbery at our mission training center."

George went on to explain that Nancy, one of our missionaries, had her suitcase and passport stolen at our new housing facility. The thieves took medical books and instruments from Dr. Rafael, one of our American doctors, and several items from the kitchen.

Stepping outside, I asked the Haitian women if they had seen anything. All of them shook their heads.

Then one of them whispered, "It's the mercy of God— the mercy of God."

I stared at her, not comprehending.

"If anyone had woken up," she continued, "the thieves would have killed them."

I shuddered. I heard that when voodoo was involved in a robbery, the thieves sprinkle a powder around the area, supposedly to keep the people from waking. Whatever the reason—perhaps because the thieves were very good at their job—all of us had slept through the entire escapade.

For the next hour several of us debated about what we should do. Some of the missionaries wanted to cancel our retreat to make a statement to the villagers that we were upset and wouldn't tolerate this sort of thing. On the other hand, did we want to stop what might be a real time of spiritual growth and renewal for these women?

After a lot of deliberation, we decided to go ahead with our plans.

Whenever I had special events, I tried to adapt the same special touches that I had learned at Women's Aglow. For example, once I had a rose fashioned out of red material on each of their name tags, and I always made sure that the table was nicely set with flowers. So after arriving at the mountain retreat, I stopped at a nearby garden shop and purchased red and white geranium plants, placing them on each table.

During the weekend, we had wonderful times of testimonies, prayer, and praise. Kelli, Mary Jane, or I taught them from the Bible. We also had lots of fun times playing games and giving away small gifts.

Early on the morning we were to leave, we were informed by the people at the Baptist mission that unexpected political demonstrations were going on. The only road to our mission was the main highway, which we knew would probably be filled with roadblocks.

Throwing our things together, we left immediately, knowing that the full fury of the demonstrations would heighten around noontime. As Mary Jane and I each drove one of our trucks into Port-au-Prince, the roads were quiet. Deserted.

Then I heard noises approaching in our direction. Glancing sideways, I stiffened. A mob was running towards us, shouting political slogans. Mary Jane and I pulled over to the side of the road.

When the demonstrators passed peaceably, I let out a sigh of relief. Even though there were still a few small road-blocks on the way home—fires that were just starting—we managed to pass them without incident.

When we returned home, George informed us that all of Dr. Rafael's stolen books and instruments had been discovered in a nearby bush; however, we never did find out who was responsible. George hired a night guard to watch over our property, and we never experienced another break-in.

The political strife, though, was far from over. Several months later on Sunday, September 11, a massacre took place in a Roman Catholic Church where Reverend Jean-Bertrand Aristide, a virulent opponent of the government, celebrated mass. During the service, Tonton Macoutes entered the church with guns and machetes and began killing people at random; they even stabbed a pregnant woman in the stomach. When they left, 11 people were dead and 77 severely wounded. That week three other churches in the city of Port-au-Prince were burned down. All of this took place because a group within the Roman Catholic Church, called *ti l'eglise* (little church), was very outspoken in their criticism of the present military government.

The people of Haiti were appalled at these atrocious acts, and on September 18, the rank and file of the military staged another coup. The new government promised freedom of the press, human rights, and democratic elections in the near future, but we knew the battle would continue indefinitely.

Meanwhile, we tried to continue focusing our energies on the tasks God had called us to. It was hard to believe that six years ago when our mission began, we started with 161 children meeting in little woven thatches along the ocean front in Bord Mer. Now we had 2,200 children in eight schools and a ninth one opening soon in Leogane. We also had 200 adults enrolled in eight literacy schools where we taught them to read and write. Two depot buildings, a dining hall, school kitchen, and office complex were in use. And soon construction would begin on our new high school building, located on the main highway near the town of Leogane.

We had a number of people employed at the mission: 83 teachers, 38 people in the school kitchen and at the missions training center, 7 night security guards and 38 men working on construction projects. We were now one of the largest employers on the Leogane Plain, which helped to boost the local economy.

My weekly women's meetings, consisting of 85 women, were also doing well. Soon two incidences occurred that knit me even closer to them.

It started on a typical Sunday morning when Olimcia—the mother of Edna who had epilepsy—rushed into our classroom where I was teaching, visibly upset. In her hands she held an old ratty towel with a small form inside. "Madam George," she said with urgency in her voice. "This is my baby girl, and I think she's going to die."

I nodded understandingly. I knew this was Olimcia's 13th baby and that she had already lost six of them.

Before I had a chance to say something, Olimcia thrust the limp baby into my arms. I felt like I was holding a small chicken. The rest of the women, aware of Olimcia's past losses, looked at me, waiting and wondering what I would do.

No one spoke. No one moved.

What I did next still surprises me. Instead of taking some kind of action, I sat there calmly, silently, gathering my thoughts. Then, shifting my attention back to my lesson, I resumed my teaching.

Twenty minutes later, after sharing about God's love and how he values us far more than the sparrows, I finally finished.

Then I opened the towel and peered inside. Immediately I saw the warning signs of death. The baby's lips were quivering and her skin was dry—indications that she was dehydrated and had only hours to live. It was then that it hit me: When there's a fire, you put it out. Why hadn't I grabbed the baby and rushed her to the hospital? By waiting, I could have easily opened the towel and found a dead baby on my lap.

I noticed George strolling by. "Honey," I yelled, "this baby is going to die. Can I take the car to the hospital?"

"Sure. But if you could find someone to nurse the baby, you would be better off."

My mind lingered over the possibility. Then I remembered that Yvette, a very faithful woman in my women's class, just had a baby the day before.

Motioning for Olimcia to follow me, I carried the baby to our car. Soon we were speeding to Neply, a half-mile away. We hurried out of the car with Olimcia close behind as I carried the baby across a log over the stream, and tried to keep my balance.

After arriving at Yvette's mud hut, we were immediately invited in. Yvette, a petite woman with an engaging smile, was lying on her bed with her newborn son next to her.

Catching my breath, my words came rushing out: "I'm wondering if God has a plan for you to save the life of

Olimcia's baby. If you're willing to nurse her and the baby's willing to nurse, this baby can live."

Yvette nodded in agreement as her hands reached out towards the baby. I gave her to Yvette, who then placed the baby to her breast.

Olimcia stood next to me, still as a stone, her eyes riveted to her baby as she gnawed her lip, waiting to see what would happen.

A strained silence filled the air. Then, a moment later, the baby sucked.

The tension drained away as my heart leapt inside. Turning to Olimcia, I saw a look of joy spread across her face as her eyes beamed with happiness. It appeared that her little baby girl would live after all.

Olimcia named her baby Jezila, meaning "Jesus is here."

Word spread quickly throughout the village of the baby's remarkable recovery, becoming a wonderful testimony of how God used Yvette to save Jezila's life. As a result, women with similar problems found other wet nurses to save the lives of their babies also.

Soon the women were reaching out to one another in other ways.

One morning, a young Haitian mother of five came in late, holding her crying baby boy. While I taught, the baby continued to cry softly in the background. As the other women taunted and teased her, the woman's embarrassment mounted.

After the meeting, I listened as one of the women—obviously annoyed—asked, "Why couldn't you keep your baby quiet?"

"He's hungry. But I don't have any money to feed him."

My heart sank. Of the 7.3 million people now living in Haiti, I knew that most of them eat only one meal a day. Some of them are forced to go days without food.

Then one of the women—the third wife of the voodoo priest—approached the mother. Reaching inside her pocket, she took out some Haitian currency and handed it to her. "Take this and buy your baby some food."

I smiled broadly as my heart warmed inside. The Haitians had always helped one another, but rarely outside their own families: They were too busy struggling just to provide for their own. But this woman had treated her as a true sister in Christ—and one who needed help.

As the months rolled by and summer approached, my heart continued to be buoyed over the women's progress. George shared my delight even as he concentrated on the construction of our new high school. Although he hoped to complete it by fall, his efforts were once again plagued by thievery. Cement, building supplies, and wheelbarrows were stolen. Finally, George had a shed built where everything could be locked up, but soon the lock was broken and everything was stolen. Soon afterwards, we hired a guard.

Meanwhile, an engineer who knew of our project from the United States Agency for International Development, asked George, "Aren't you afraid that during a political upheaval your school will be destroyed?"

I knew that the engineer's fears were well-grounded. When the Haitians first won their independence, they responded by completely destroying the wealth of their country—including their irrigation systems and plantations. Even now, political enemies often had their houses burned down and their harvests destroyed.

George decided to take no chances. Once the high school was built, he hired two more guards. Even though they only carried machetes and certainly couldn't fend off a mob, at least we had no problems with thievery after that. It was also a good investment since the cost of replacing just one school chair was the same as hiring a guard for six months.

Meanwhile, Yolene—the young woman who had been out of her mind for so many years and now claimed she was

converted—asked to be admitted into our high school program. I was still very skeptical, unsure of her motives. Our
high school was reserved for only those with the highest
grades and commitment to God. But Yolene was still unwilling to renounce Satan in her life.

"How can we let her in?" I asked George. "We're trying to have a Christian environment and there she'll be, having contortions and throwing herself on the floor. It'll just
make trouble for everyone."

"No," George responded firmly. "She's made a confession of faith. She needs to be in our Christian high school
so she can be completely delivered."

After Yolene was accepted into our high school,
George soon proved to be right. The environment brought
further conviction in her life. By the end of the first semester, she not only surrendered herself completely to God but
began openly sharing her faith with anyone who listened.
Now, at the crossroads where she once spent many hours
tearing at her hair and trying to drown herself, she could be
found singing and giving testimonies of her deliverance.

As the months flew by, my family was experiencing
changes of their own. Charlie was attending Columbia Bible
College in Columbia, South Carolina, and planned on
spending the summer in Haiti with us. Timothy had just
returned to Worcester where he lived with George, Jr., finishing up his last year of high school there. Although we
would miss him, his private instrument lessons to the
Haitians had paid off. One of our young Haitians was playing the piano at our church in Bord Mer.

In October of 1989, George and I were in
Massachusetts for a breakfast meeting where we gave an
update to our supporters about our mission's progress. One
of the pastors who planned on attending—a longtime friend
of my husband's—never showed up. Later we found out that
his only daughter, just 22 years old, had been killed by a
drunk driver.

My heart ached for him. Here was a man who lived in the United States, had the best hospitals and technology available, and yet none of it was able to save her. *God,* I said silently, *from now on I'll never complain again about being unable to watch over my children. You have shut my mouth forever.*

A few weeks later, God blessed me in a special way with my family. When George, Jr. came for his yearly visit to Haiti, he met one of our new missionaries, a pretty blue-eyed young woman named Paula. Soon they were corresponding back and forth as their relationship became more serious. By spring, George, Jr. and Paula decided to get married. The wedding was set for September 1, 1990. What fun it was for me to be in on their courtship and engagement. It was an added blessing since I never imagined I would get a chance to know a future daughter-in-law of mine now that I no longer lived in the States.

Meanwhile, Kelli, now 30, was frustrated over her lack of potential suitors in Haiti. To encourage her, I gave her a piece of white lace for Christmas. Then I told her to put it out on her dresser where she could see it so she would be reminded to trust God for a husband.

Two weeks later, a man named Rob asked her to attend a wedding with him. A serious, hard-working missionary, he was director of a mission not far from where we were located. Soon their friendship grew into something much more serious.

While romance was in the air, George and I flew to Massachusetts in early May, just four months before George, Jr. and Paula's wedding. It was there I experienced another physical setback.

It happened in Boston, shortly after George had finished an evening speaking engagement. After the meeting, we picked up a pizza with our son, Timothy, and headed for home in George, Jr.'s white Oldsmobile. As George slowed down to 45 mph to exit off of the expressway, I removed my seat belt to put a cassette in the tape player. Just then Timothy yelled out, "Dad, you better step on it. There's a big truck ready to ram into you."

In an instant I was thrown up against the dashboard and jerked back into my seat.

Cradling my head in my hand, I felt excruciating pain. Despite the fact that our vehicle would not start, George and Timothy were completely unhurt.

Meanwhile, I couldn't lift my head. For the next hour and a half, Timothy tried to flag down a policeman until a patrol car finally showed up. The tow truck operator who hit us was apparently uninjured. He helped repair our car enough to get it started. Although he was speeding, he explained that he didn't see us slow down, therefore plowing into the back of our vehicle.

"We need to call an ambulance for Mom," I could hear Timothy saying to his father.

"Let's just see if we can get her to Worcester."

Arriving home an hour later, I could not remove my hand from supporting my head without experiencing horrible agony. Finally, at 1:00 A.M., George took me to the emergency room where I was given a series of x-rays. Finding nothing wrong, I was placed in a neck collar and given pain medication.

One week later, George and I returned to Haiti. Despite the fact that I was still experiencing considerable pain, I promised Kelli—who was now being courted seriously by Rob—that I would take her to a women's retreat in Miami for a time of refreshment. So, after flying to Miami two weeks later, I had a doctor give me another x-ray. This time I was informed that I had a fractured rib, explaining why I hurt so much.

Soon I was wearing a brace around my rib cage. But because the roads are horribly bumpy in Haiti, I felt as though I was refracturing my rib every time I traveled to different women's meetings to speak. Kelli helped as much as possible while I tried to heal. She oversaw my kitchen responsibilities for me. And since I could no longer do letter writing or even put postage stamps on envelopes since the pain shot up into my shoulder each time I tried, I concentrated on learning the computer instead.

Besides the physical pain I was experiencing, I realized that the emotional stress was taking its toll on me as well. It was good to have Charlie back for the summer, but Kelli had just announced that she was getting married to Rob in January. They planned to work together at Rob's mission. As happy as I was for her, everything inside of me ached as I thought of having to let her go.

The summer flew by quickly and soon it was time for us to attend George, Jr. and Paula's wedding. By this time, however, I was still unable to move my arm, shoulder, head or right side and was experiencing breathing difficulties. Besides this, my back hurt so bad that I had to have help zipping up my dress on the day they were married. I couldn't even frost the fruitcakes I had made for their rehearsal dinner; someone else had to volunteer for the job.

The next few months slowed to a crawl as I battled with constant pain. In October I went into Port-au-Prince with a cold face cloth wrapped around my neck to help ease the agony I felt. There I made further contacts with several agencies I was working with who were assisting our mission with food, educational materials, and building supplies. Since I found the pain unbearable because of the bumpy road conditions, I was unable to return, and I eventually lost all of my wonderful contacts with these people.

On December 19, just a few weeks before Kelli's wedding, George and I returned to Worcester to spend Christmas there for the first time in seven years. Although Mary Ann was unable to be there, it was wonderful to be with the rest of my family for the holidays. My sagging spirits rejuvenated.

While we were gone, a democratic election took place in Haiti. Four hundred non-armed security advisers from the United Nations were placed throughout the voting stations to provide protection for the voters and to make sure that the election process was observed. By now, 78 percent of the voting population had registered to vote, anxious to begin the process of establishing democracy in their country. Although there were elements of the old Duvalierist regime who wanted to disrupt the voting, Jean-Bertrand Aristide—a former Roman Catholic priest—was duly elected president of Haiti for the next five years. We heard that there was much dancing in the streets as euphoria filled the country. How we prayed that this would be a new day for Haiti, and that the country would finally stabilize and begin to make progress.

Shortly after Christmas, George returned to Haiti while Timothy, George, Jr., Paula, and I drove up to Long Island, New York, to attend Kelli and Rob's wedding. It would be a day mixed with joy and sadness for me. Not only had she been my nurse, confidante, and best friend, she had become like a daughter to me. Aware that Kelli had struggled also, I tried to put on a brave front to help her make the break from me so that she would be free to attach herself to another ministry. As I watched her go down the aisle in her long, white, satin gown, I realized that Kelli was embarking on a new life—and a new adventure altogether.

The following morning, I lay in bed as the sunlight filtered into my room in Worcester, easing my chill a little. Breathing in the cold, winter air, I noticed that my lungs felt achy and sore. Then I heard a gurgling sound in my chest and a twinge of panic shot through me. I was afraid that my lungs had filled with fluid and that I had pneumonia again.

Immediately I saw the doctor and handed him all my medical records. Since I needed to return to Haiti the next morning, I requested medicine right away.

A few hours later, I received a phone call from my husband, explaining that the situation in Haiti had worsened. Political enemies were now at war with one another more than ever before, destroying one another's fields and homes and sometimes each other, along with their children. And recently, a house next to our mission, which had been occupied by a political enemy of the present government, had been targeted for destruction.

George went on to explain that a mob of 100 angry people had come with machetes, sticks, and gasoline. And because the house was situated so close to our property, the mob had threatened to burn down our mission as well, assuming we must be a political enemy.

Fortunately, George was able to gather many of our Haitian Christian workers to speak on our behalf. He was able to convince them not to destroy the politician's home, although many in the mob threatened to return.

For the first time, I felt like quitting, sinking into a melancholic dialogue with myself. How could I return to Haiti when I was in chronic pain from my accident, could hardly breathe, had just lost my best friend, and didn't even have Timothy and Charlie with me anymore? Even Mary Jane, who was with us for four years, had just started a 6-month sabbatical, leaving me without a nurse when I returned. And now, if that wasn't enough, a mob was threatening to return and destroy our mission.

Why should I go back? I asked myself over and over. *So that I could be killed for some political beliefs I never had?*

For the first time I realized that when I made the decision to become a missionary, it had happened in my comfortable home church with music playing in the background. Then, when I finally arrived on the mission field after dreaming about it for so long, everything was an adventure. It didn't bother me that part of my family wasn't there and that I could no longer attend birthdays, holidays, and other important events; all I ever asked God to do was to bless my children in my absence. It didn't bother me that I couldn't just pick up the phone and call loved ones—that was a small price to pay for the rewards of being on the front lines and seeing lives transformed by the power of Jesus.

Yet now that I was sick, lonely, and tired of the constant political upheaval, the ecstasy of being a missionary was wearing off, causing me to wonder: *Could God really trust me with the physical and emotional pain I was experiencing?* As much as I loved Haiti and the call of missions on my life, I found it increasingly difficult to say goodbye to my family to face an uncertain future, especially in my weakened condition.

However, I knew what I had to do. Even though God is certainly not a taskmaster, the desire to serve Him was still so encompassing in my life that I knew I really had only one choice—and that was to return to Haiti and do all that I could for His Kingdom. Even though I was sick, there was such greater pain and suffering in Haiti that it all seemed relative, making me feel I should return as soon as possible.

As I surrendered myself anew, I experienced an in-filling of hope, a reassurance that God had not let go of my hand, and never would. Now, more than ever before, I knew I would have to rely upon His strength and grace to walk with me along the journey, trusting in His goodness, His faithfulness, and His provision for me—just as He had always done in the past.

Chapter 20

My Redeemer

At the Boston airport a few days later, I dragged myself to my designated gate, too weak to even hold my own carry-on bag. There I met up with Nancy, the older missionary who was previously robbed at our mission. She was bravely returning for another few weeks of short-term service.

"I'm so sick," I explained as I struggled to breathe. "I have pneumonia again, but I'm taking medicine."

"You shouldn't go in your condition."

"There's so much trouble—I have to go."

Yet, after we flew into Miami, we were informed that all flights to Port-au-Prince had been canceled because of the attempted hijacking of an American Airlines flight. In the meantime, we would have to check with the airport each day to find out when flights would resume flying again.

After encouraging Nancy to return to Boston, I stayed with my daughter Mary Ann, who was still attending school in Miami. There I tried to rest as much as possible.

After several days, I finally saw the doctor who diagnosed my fractured rib. "Are you feeling any better since taking your medicine?"

"A little," I replied, trying to sound convincing.

Despite my physical condition, I was able to fly to Haiti just one week later. Aware that our vehicle's air conditioning wasn't working and that we would probably have to go through several roadblocks before arriving at our mission, I planned ahead by taking along a mask with me.

Now as I scanned the jammed airport, I didn't see George anywhere. Instead, I was met by Ken, a senior pastor friend of ours who was visiting along with some of his church members.

"Where's George?" I asked, trying to keep the fear out of my voice.

Ken's voice was soft and distant. "I'll tell you all about it once we get in the truck."

Too weak to argue, I placed the mask over my face. Then, as we made our way outside into the smoggy, oppressive air, I tried to steady my labored breathing.

Once inside our truck, Ken explained that the mob who had previously threatened our mission was supposed to return today. This time, George wasn't sure he could keep them from destroying our neighbor's property or our own.

Perspiration soaked through my dress as horrible thoughts of the future took hold: the mission destroyed. George killed. Me dead from pneumonia. Feeling emotionally and physically exhausted and unable to think clearly, I fell silent.

As Ken sped along the highway, I noticed signs of earlier roadblocks as we passed by piles of smoldering tires and pieces of car wreckage. Fortunately, we had no problem arriving safely at our mission a few hours later.

Stepping out of the truck, I was relieved to see that everything was still intact. Then I spotted George bounding towards me. As he came closer, I could see deep circles under his eyes as he gave me a tight squeeze. "The mob just left," he explained. "Hundreds of our villagers persuaded them that we had no connection with any political party; we only wanted to feed and educate their children."

For the first time since landing in Haiti, I felt my face visibly relax. Soon I was resting inside the comfort of our home.

Yet as I struggled to get better, Haiti's situation continued to decline. Aristide, now the new president, had promised to increase wages and bring down the price of goods in the country, especially food. Instead, the cost of everything had gone up, wages remained the same, and unemployment was at an all-time high.

Although the poor people of Haiti were for Aristide, the middle and upper classes were not. Once again, the country was divided and unwilling to compromise, making it difficult to move forward.

The next month passed by in a blur. At least twice a day, after sleeping 10 to 12 hours at night, I was forced to return to bed, constantly battling chills, fever, weakness, and other flu-like symptoms. While others took over most of my responsibilities, I managed to continue with my weekly women's meetings. Often I spoke to the women about healing, afterwards praying for those who were sick and trying to trust God for my own healing as well. But as much as I wanted to get well, to function again and be useful, I felt no signs of improvement.

Even George was discouraged, feeling helpless and uncomfortable around me. I was aware that he always had a hard time dealing with sickness, and my spirits sank even deeper.

George, Jr. did nothing to brighten my outlook either. Upset over all the constant medical attention I required, especially since he ended up looking after me most of the time, he finally scrawled me a letter: "I'm so tired of all of your medical crises," he wrote, "that I took out a big fat life insurance policy on you." Fortunately, he had already taken out health insurance on me as well.

Even my son's anger could not will me to get better. In early March—after I was sick for two months—George, Jr. came for his annual visit. Alarmed at my pale appearance and the fact that the hospital was unable to find out what was wrong with me, my take-charge son finally announced, "If you're not feeling better by the time I leave, you're coming home with me."

A few days later I flew to our home in Worcester where George, Jr., Paula, and Timothy were all living. During the next three weeks I had all sorts of tests taken at the hospital while Paula took royal care of me, encouraging me to eat and rest as much as possible. When the test results were all in, I was diagnosed with acute chronic mononucleosis. Like a long-term virus that doesn't go away, the only treatment for it is rest and good nutrition—stress being the number one enemy. And unless I took care of my health, I was told that I would continue to have lapses. In the meantime, the doctor was unable to give me any timetable for my recovery.

The days dragged by as I continued to battle chills, headaches, fever, fatigue, and nausea. It was as though a dark gray fog had settled over me, wrapping itself around me and squeezing out all the light. I contacted almost no one in the area, too ashamed to let my friends know how I was feeling. Only my parents were regular visitors, honoring my request to keep my condition quiet.

Two weeks after returning home, I was standing in the hospital foyer waiting for a ride when I felt a tap on my shoulder. "Is that you, Jeanne?"

Spinning around, I was startled to see Dan Curtis, a friend of ours for 15 years and pastor of a large interdenominational church. His wife, along with others in his church, had served on my Women's Aglow Board, and both George and I had many friends in his congregation.

Nodding, I straightened my shoulders, trying to look as normal as possible. "I'm home from Haiti. I've been a little sick."

After Dan expressed his sympathy and prayers for my recovery, he headed down the corridor. I stood there, watching him in the distance, feeling ashamed and miserable. Now that he knew my secret, I was glad he wasn't supporting our mission. I would really have been embarrassed. Imagine, a missionary you're helping who can't even work.

During the next few days, I cried out to God, asking Him to cut out anything in me that could be hindering my recovery. As I waited, I finally concluded that perhaps it wasn't sin at all; perhaps I simply could no longer push myself emotionally and physically like I had done in the past. My memory replayed the admonition I received from a pastor years ago at Camp Woodhaven: "You're working too hard. Your body's going to break down." Chronic mononucleosis, I knew, was often a result of stress, usually occurring in young people going off to college and having a difficult time adjusting to the pressures. Now, for the first time, I was forced to take stock of the stresses in my own life. Besides the constant stress of an ever-changing missionary team as well as the political strife going on in Haiti, I realized my body had been further weakened from the car accident and the subsequent stress of no longer being as productive.

In the past, I had always loved sweets, preferring chocolate to chicken. Yet I realized that I couldn't expect God to take care of me if I wasn't willing to take care of myself. Now I actually wanted to drink carrot juice.

I was also learning to rest in His love and enjoy our fellowship together even when I couldn't do anything for Him. But at times it was still difficult. Often, I found myself praying, "Lord, please make this time count for the people of Haiti."

One week after I had run into Dan Curtis at the hospital, Paula poked her head into my bedroom where I was propped up on my pillow, busy memorizing Psalm 40. "Pastor Curtis is on the phone," she explained. "He wants to know if you're well enough to talk."

Nodding my consent, Paula handed me the phone.

After a quick greeting, Dan got right to the point. "Next week we're having a mission board meeting. Do you think you can talk to us about your ministry in Haiti?"

"I'll trust God to help me," I responded. For the first time I felt a glimmer of hope. Maybe God would use me during my recuperation after all.

George, Jr. and Timothy shared in my enthusiasm over this new opportunity, for we were always looking for ways to help the Haitians. Now that Dan's church members would get a chance to learn about our ministry, perhaps they, too, could be another channel to bless the children of Haiti.

As the big day finally arrived, however, I felt devoid of energy. Even after resting all morning, I wondered how I was going to manage. Reclining the front seat of the car as far back as possible, I closed my eyes and prayed while Timothy drove the 7-miles to the church.

After 10 minutes, we pulled up in front of a beautiful white colonial structure in a middle-class suburb. After Timothy helped me in, I was ushered to a small room where Pastor Curtis and the others were seated around a large, oblong table.

Taking a seat, I swallowed hard, as nine well-dressed and educated people waited to hear what I had to say. I felt honored to be there, yet I was afraid I might not represent the people of Haiti very well, especially in my weakened condition. My mouth felt parched and dry while the rest of me was bathed in a film of sweat; my limbs felt heavy, as though I couldn't move.

Gathering my courage, I prayed for the strength to speak. Soon I found myself comfortably sharing about the purpose and progress of our mission. Afterwards, I answered the committee's questions.

It was all over in thirty minutes. I felt completely drained, but I could tell by the interest on people's faces that it had gone well. But no matter whether the church decided to support our ministry or not, I felt rejuvenated in my spirit, just by doing something useful again.

A few days later, despite still feeling horrible, I had even more cause for celebration after Paula came bounding into my room. A look of joy spread across her face as she exclaimed, "I just took a test and I'm pregnant!"

I brightened noticeably. Propping myself up in bed, I motioned for her to come towards me. Then, placing my hand on her stomach, I prayed that God would bless her baby and that I would live to see my first grandchild. Looking back, I feel I may have been a bit melodramatic, but at the time I really wasn't sure I was going to make it.

After two long months, however, I was still very much alive and had made a complete recovery, allowing me to return to Haiti. Just before I left, I received news that Pastor Dan's church had decided to generously support our mission. How grateful I was that God had redeemed my situation and used it to ultimately feed and educate more Haitian children.

∞ ∞ ∞ ∞ ∞

Shortly after I returned to Haiti, Charlie announced that he was getting married to Rachel, a young woman he met in college. Trained as a physical therapist, Rachel had been raised by missionary parents in India. How thrilled I was that my future daughter-in-law was born and grew up in the country that I loved so deeply—she even had the same round brown eyes and straight long brown hair of that of the Indian people.

Because Rachel's parents were in the States for only a short furlough, they decided to get married on June 15, just a few weeks away. By then, Charlie and Rachel would have graduated from Columbia Bible College with B.A. degrees in Bible and Missions. After they married, they agreed to come to Haiti and work with us.

Two days before the wedding, George and I flew to Greenville, South Carolina, for the big event. The wedding went off beautifully, except that Mary Ann was suffering from severe anemia. After the reception, she was so weak we put her on an early plane to Miami to see her doctor.

The next night, 30 minutes before George was to speak at a church, I phoned Mary Ann, who was now in the hospital, to see how she was doing. Sounding weak and distant, she explained that she already had two blood transfusions and that they were considering one more. Later, I shared a testimony and George preached, but my heart ached throughout the meeting for my only daughter.

The following morning, George woke up with a high temperature, sick with prostatitis. Despite his illness, I knew he had to drive down to Virginia Beach the next day. Suddenly I was torn: Should I leave George to be with Mary Ann?

Finally I told my daughter, "I'll send you the money I would have spent to fly to Miami and stay with your father."

When I called Mary Ann from Virginia Beach the next day, she was still hospitalized, her voice sad and withdrawn. Soon she was given a third and fourth blood transfusion.

On July 3, George and I flew into Miami on our return trip to Haiti. George had fully recovered after being on antibiotics, and Mary Ann was recuperating at home.

Mary Ann met us at the Miami airport to say goodbye. Her long, light-brown hair framed a drawn and pale face, and she had a yellowish color to her skin. After 15 precious minutes together, I found my resolve weakening as I hugged her tightly and said goodbye. Stifling a sob that was threatening to surface, I turned away.

As I boarded the plane along with George, regret flooded through me as I thought of my daughter, all alone in Miami, with no family nearby. Why hadn't I asked one of our sons to be with my husband so I could have been with her?

Standing in the back of the airplane, I cried for my daughter—the deepest, darkest, most painful tears I had ever—could ever—shed. When a stewardess asked me what was wrong, I sobbed, "I've just said goodbye to my daughter...and it's so painful. She's been sick, and I wasn't with her when she needed me." How hard it was to leave her again.

At least I had Charlie back with us in Haiti, along with his new bride Rachel. And Mary Jane had also returned from her furlough. Not only was she a nurse and hard worker, but she had a knowledge of the Haitian culture, making her extremely valuable to our mission.

Haiti's political situation, however, continued to darken. In September, after Aristide had been in office for only seven and a half months, he was suddenly ousted by a General named Cedras. Hoping to pressure the new government into letting Aristide return, the United States was now enforcing an embargo against the country.

On November 21, I returned to Worcester to visit my first grandson, whom George and Paula had named Michael. Although I hoped to be there in time for his birth, I received the news two days later because of difficulties in communication. Nevertheless, it was wonderful to see my little dark-haired, olive-skinned grandson as well as his proud parents. It was also great to visit again with Mary Ann, who was feeling herself again.

After I returned to Haiti, I was still tempted to worry sometimes about my growing family. However, I knew I had to continually choose to surrender them into God's care, trusting Him to watch over them in my absence. Besides, in comparison to the Haitians' plight, I realized it was a small sacrifice to pay. And, as God gave me the grace to be away from my children, He also gave me a greater love for the people He had called me to serve in Haiti. Also, because of the physical suffering I had been through, I found that whenever any of them suffered now, I could empathize to a much greater degree.

It was especially hard the day I heard about the terrible suffering of one little girl who had become so very special to me....

Chapter 21

The Suffering of the Innocent

The oppressive summer heat bore down upon me as I sat in my office, trying to tackle the stack of correspondence in front of me. A dingy-looking fan rattled, moving the air only a little, yet easing my discomfort somewhat.

Then, above the noisy fan, I heard a tap at the window. Perturbed, I looked up to see Frantz, one of our students, and Edna's older brother, the little girl who had epilepsy. Didn't he know that the office was already closed?

Stepping outside into the bright sunlight, I exchanged irritation for concern as I noticed a solemn expression on Frantz' features, his dark brow creased with worry.

Soon his words came tumbling out: "Edna's dying. She's been having seizures."

I looked at Frantz and questioned him about Edna's condition. Edna had been on medication for years and had been completely free from seizures. Now that school was out, it was much more difficult to check on our students to make sure they were taking their medicine. If her mother, Olimcia, hadn't bothered to come to the clinic and get her supply refilled…

A cold shiver ran through me. I was especially concerned because I knew that Olimcia—a highly nervous individual—had recently lost her second husband and was struggling to take care of her seven healthy children. Besides that, her teenage daughter, Gertrude, had two children who were living with Olimcia as well.

A short time later, I hastened to Olimcia's hut, which was located in a secluded area in the village of Neply. As I approached, I noticed Olimcia, bent over a few sweet potatoes she was cooking inside a rusted pan, which was sitting on top of three stones. Several of her children encircled the small fire, waiting until they could finally eat.

As soon as Olimcia saw me, surprise registered on her face. I explained that I was there to see Edna. Olimcia lowered her eyes and nodded, replying that she wasn't doing well. Then, motioning toward the hut, she encouraged me to go in.

I stepped inside, my heart breaking into a hundred pieces as I noticed 13-year-old Edna, lying off to one side on a thin mat with a dirty sheet over her body; I could see her little hip bones sticking out. It was obvious that she was at the point of starving to death.

The cold, awful truth hit me full force, something not all that uncommon in a family that was barely surviving. I knew that children are a Haitian's riches—helping to work in the fields and take care of them in their old age—but Olimcia had obviously reached the end of her rope. Being illiterate and feeling that Edna had no future, she stopped her medication. As a result, Edna's seizures had begun again. It also appeared that Olimcia had stopped feeding her, having made a conscious decision to let her daughter die.

When I whispered Edna's name, she turned slightly and half-opened her sunken, disconsolate eyes for a moment. Then, as I talked about how much God loved her, she nodded her head in understanding.

With no time to lose I hustled home, returning quickly with a visiting American doctor.

After the doctor examined her, he took me aside, explaining it was too late to save her. Nevertheless, he valiantly tried building her up with fluids in the faint hope that she might pull through. Gazing at Edna with an aching heart, I prayed for a miracle.

The following morning I visited Edna again as she held on tenaciously to life. Sitting beside her on the dirt floor, I sang several songs that she had learned in school. One in particular, I repeated over and over again in Creole: *Mwen konnen Bondye la* (I know God is here) to hear me, To take my burdens and stress. He shares my load with me... Even though I have a lot of problems and a heavy load to carry, I have confidence His grace is sufficient. And I know God is here.

After I finished, Edna seemed to rally as the words became like a healing balm, ministering comfort and encouragement to her.

The next day when I visited, Edna had been moved to an area mainly used for cooking. Open on all sides, it had a simple straw covering on top. Barely conscious, she lay there, unmoving, while her sister, Gertrude, kept watch. Aware that Gertrude was a dedicated Christian, I announced, "Get your hymnal. I want us to sing a song to Edna." After Gertrude fetched her hymnal from the mud hut, she stood beside me and turned the pages to a song.

Just as we were about to start, Edna drew her last breath—and died.

Gertrude flinched noticeably. "Let's still sing," I said resolutely.

Gertrude nodded weakly, then we raised our voices in unison: "Until death, we'll be faithful to You, Until death, You will be our King...Yes, we will die, fighting the good fight of faith."

Gertrude's eyes brimmed with tears, and her voice shook as she struggled to continue: "Until death! This is our battle cry, The free cry of a redeemed people.... "

When the song ended, Gertrude uttered the death cry—a spine-chilling, high-pitched shriek of agony. Quickly, crowds of people burst onto the scene, wailing uncontrollably.

Edna's mother was inconsolable as she cried along with the rest of her grieving friends and relatives, and I knew she would miss Edna greatly. Although it appeared that Olimcia's decision to let her daughter die was heartless, I was no longer as quick to judge or to give my "if-that-were-me" analysis to suffering people. I was also aware that because Olimcia was illiterate, recently widowed, and constantly struggling to survive from day to day, the combination had finally taken its toll on her.

Gazing up toward heaven, I saw a "Madam Sara," a yellow-feathered bird about the size of a sparrow. It reminded me of the Scripture in Matthew 6 that tells us that we are of much greater value to our Heavenly Father than the birds of the air.

Shifting my eyes back to Edna again—her face finally at peace—I pictured her in God's arms now, resting securely in His love.

Because I wanted Edna's funeral to be as lovely as possible to honor her short life, I searched through a few wedding dresses that had been donated to us. Among the pile was a beautiful, long, white formal gown, covered with layers of lace. I gathered some silk pastel roses I had been saving.

Draping the dress over my arm and holding the roses in my other hand, I hastened to Neply. Already the mortician was there, measuring Edna's body with a tree branch in order to construct a casket to fit her exactly. Wood was costly and there couldn't be any waste. I handed him my things, instructing him how to place the flowers in Edna's hands, with her fingers wrapped around them.

The next day, while we waited for the casket to arrive, other villagers wandered in and out of the already cramped yard. Then out of the corner of one eye, I watched with disbelief as a young girl, about 9 years old, crept up to Edna's body and snatched a couple of roses from her hand.

Memories of Rodrigues' brother, Michelet, who stripped Rodrigues of his school uniform before he was buried, flashed through my mind. Even in death, I realized, nothing was sacred. The only rule was survival.

A long, oppressive afternoon labored past as I waited for the casket, along with an American visitor and everyone else who had gathered. Finally, after three hours, we ambled back to our mission, even though the funeral hadn't started.

Later I discovered that it took several more hours before the casket arrived and Edna was finally buried. I'll never know if any of her roses were buried with her.

∞ ∞ ∞ ∞ ∞

Life for most Haitians continued to deteriorate. During the next year, while Aristide resided in the United States, the embargo remained in effect, disrupting an already fragile economy. As proposals, counter proposals, promises, and constant changes in government abounded, Haiti's infrastructure was breaking down. The Haitians had lost 50,000 factory jobs near the airport in Port-au-Prince because nothing was being transported in or out of the country. And while unemployment soared to over 80 percent, prices escalated even further, creating terrible suffering for those not rich enough to deal on the black market. Items such as propane gas, animal feed, and baby chicks were sometimes not even available. A bar of soap that cost 22 cents a year ago was now 60 cents.

Our local hospital was affected by the embargo, and quickly ran out of supplies. One of our village women who was in our prenatal program suffering from a complicated pregnancy, died three days after delivering a baby girl because no blood was available for her. Not only was there no blood, even if there had been, there weren't even the plastic bags to store the blood. The baby's aunt took care of her, and I visited little Rosie as often as I could, becoming a kind of surrogate grandmother to her.

The United States policy towards Haiti affected our mission in other ways as well, making it far more costly to build. Until recently, cement was being sold for $11 a sack—now it had soared to $56 a sack. Medicine had also doubled, and sometimes even tripled, in price. Then, an American agency that supplied food to our school children via an international agency said that they could no longer help because it would show they supported the present regime. Once again, we had to trust God to meet our needs.

Soon I felt ashamed to be an American. Whenever anyone asked me my nationality, I apologized for the suffering we were causing them. But the response was always the same: How can you make innocent people die? Now, because of the embargo and the subsequent fear of retribution, it was a tense time for any Americans living in Haiti, and many were beginning to leave.

With no stable government in place, terrible crimes continued to be committed. Churches in America became reluctant to send their young people to work with us, redirecting them into other countries that were safer. And who could blame them? Why should a pastor send 50 young people into a country that could erupt into political violence at any moment?

Although the embargo had been in effect for nine months, God was not hindered from His work and He still continued to bless us at NEW Missions, where we had 16 missionaries serving with us. Charlie and Rachel, however, would be leaving for Boston in July—just two months away—since Rachel was now pregnant, expecting a baby August 1. During their stay, Charlie planned to work at Camp Woodhaven and minister in churches throughout New England, then return to Haiti with Rachel and the baby in September.

We now had 3,000 children enrolled in our schools, making it necessary to build a 3,200 square-foot food depot since our storage areas were inadequate for our growing student population. And recently, our high school had been inspected, approved, and licensed by the Haitian government. Our 10 primary schools were already licensed for several years.

For a long time at NEW Missions, we talked about the need of having a ham radio. Finally George got his amateur license, allowing him to speak with other missionaries in Haiti, making it far easier to receive news and to get help in case of an emergency. He also set up a tower and antenna for us to communicate with our friends and family back in the United States. Several missionaries on our team were studying for their amateur licenses as well.

Meanwhile, my women's ministry had continued to prosper. We had 11 weekly women's meetings in our area, and there were 40 women who wanted to be trained to lead groups in their own villages. Now that God had touched these women's hearts, they were obediently responding to His call of evangelism.

On June 3, I invited the pastor's wives and women leaders from churches all over the Leogane area—including Episcopalians, Baptists, and Nazarenes—to come together in celebration of my 50th birthday.

Forty Haitian women, plus a dozen Americans representing several other churches and mission groups in the area, sat together in our dining room facility—built at our mission training center. Beside each place setting was a beautifully painted basket, containing silk flowers and rolls.

After the women were served a dinner of fried chicken, beans, rice, and birthday cake, I gave them a short message on the love of Jesus, and then told them of our first interdenominational women's meeting in July, just seven weeks away. It would be much like the meetings I was involved with in Women's Aglow, where everyone came together to sing, share testimonies, and pray.

On July 28, women packed into a church that was led by Pastor Emmanuel, director of our primary school in Signeau. He was also serving as advisor and facilitator for our women's ministry. Six hundred women were present, each bearing a name tag with a number written on it.

Despite the brutal summer heat, everyone was in high spirits as they chatted over cake and cold drinks. Next, we had a tremendous time of praise and worship as tambourines played in the background. Then, after several moving testimonies and powerful preaching by an American-Haitian woman, many thronged forward for prayer and personal ministry. At the close of the meeting, I drew five numbers. As each winner came forward, the other women clapped. The winners received a gift of sheets, towels, pots, or pans that visitors had donated to our mission.

I felt like a miracle had taken place. Not only had Haitians from different churches united for the first time, but Americans from different missions as well, dispelling barriers and feelings of mistrust that had been harbored for years. Even my own struggles with the Haitian women and the offenses I first felt when I arrived here seemed light years behind me. Now, not only did I feel deep unshakable bonds with these women, but the women's ministry was expanding in ways I never dreamed possible.

Our family soon expanded as well. On August 7, Rachel gave birth to a baby boy, whom she and Charlie named Nathan. Meanwhile, Charlie decided to remain as pastor of The Chapel at Camp Woodhaven for a while rather than return to Haiti as planned. Although George and I would miss them both, I was glad they were doing so well.

Little did we know that our family's faith and trust in God was about to be severely tested.

Chapter 22

The Accident

It was 6:00 A.M. as I wiped the sleep from my eyes, anticipating the day's events. It was September 22, and this afternoon we were having our second interdenominational women's meeting.

Despite the fact that I was in high spirits, a frightening, evil presence seemed to have settled in my room. It seemed eerily cold. Dark. Then, while showering, I experienced a sharp pain in one of my upper back teeth, even though I never had a problem with that tooth before.

Was the tooth simply a bad sign of things to come? Was Satan unhappy with the progress we were making with the Haitian women?

Lifting my chin, I felt a hard knot of resolve form in my stomach as I pushed down my fears and slipped on a short-sleeved blue, cotton dress. As I concentrated on arranging my brown hair into a bun, I determined that a toothache wouldn't interfere with the afternoon's events. The pain left within an hour, but I struggled with a growing sense of foreboding just beneath the surface.

The morning flew by as I directed a few Haitian workers in various tasks and made preparations for the meeting at 2 :00 P.M. Around noon, George approached me, a quiet concern in his eyes. He had just received word from a mission down the road that owned a telephone that one of our sons had been in a serious car accident. He explained that there was no further information available yet; they didn't even know which one of our sons was involved. In order to obtain more information, George would have to do a radio patch.

My mouth dropped open as I stared at my husband wordlessly. Soon a dull buzz filled my head as all the fears I had pushed down stirred and surfaced again.

Just before the women's meeting was scheduled to begin, George managed to get in touch with our daughter-in-law, Paula. She explained that Charlie, Rachel, and their 6-week old son, Nathan, had been involved in a car accident on their way from South Carolina to a college reunion near Boston. Apparently, Charlie had been driving for 15 hours and was looking for a rest area when he fell asleep at the wheel. Now Charlie was in one hospital with a back injury while Rachel—who was unharmed—was on her way to another hospital with Nathan, who was suffering from a severe head injury.

Aware that Rachel's parents were both in India, I longed to jump on the next plane headed for Miami. But how could I stop today's meeting just because of my own personal trauma? People had already walked long distances to come, many needing encouragement and personal ministry themselves.

Instead, I drew a deep breath, trying to let out all the anxiety that was bottled up inside of me. As tears clouded my vision, I prayed, "Lord Jesus, you know how much I want to be with Charlie, Rachel, and Nathan right now. Yet, I realize this ministry must take place today. So You be by their side…It's better than me."

When the meeting began, I sat with the rest of the women, feeling completely numb, devoid of all energy and emotion. Soon a missionary appeared on the stage and explained to the women what had happened to my son and family, so they would understand why I wasn't participating. I sensed a real love and empathy from this crowd: Suffering was one thing the Haitians understood very well.

Standing quietly as the others sang—my expression sad and withdrawn—the reality of what had taken place began to hit me head-on, challenging my faith and trust in God to watch over my children. As fear crashed upon me, I felt overwhelmed by the possible outcome of the accident. My mind shot back to the declaration I had made to the Lord three years earlier, promising never to complain about living in Haiti where I couldn't be there and protect my children. Would I be able to honor that commitment now?

I slumped down into a chair as the meeting continued in a blur. My thoughts grew fuzzy and distant. When it was all over, several women expressed their concern and commitment to pray for my family. I retreated to my house, feeling helpless, yet trying to trust God in this dire situation.

The next day George, Jr. phoned. He had driven up to Newburg, New York, where the accident had occurred and picked up Charlie, who was discharged from the hospital and was recovering well from a slight back injury. George, Jr. had taken Charlie to see Rachel and Nathan and was now calling to fill us in on Nathan's condition. He explained that Nathan had two skull fractures and was bleeding from his brain. He had also had three serious seizures.

George, Jr. also shared with me a strange experience he had had. On the morning of the accident, at 6:00 A.M., he jolted from sleep, feeling an evil presence in his bedroom while hearing a loud noise, like that of screeching metal and shattering glass. Jumping out of bed, he woke his wife, Paula, and looked out the window, thinking someone must have crashed their vehicle into their home. Instead there was nothing. No one.

For the next hour, George, Jr. shook and trembled. Then he received word that Charlie and Rachel had been in a car accident at exactly 6:00 A.M., the same time he was awakened from sleep by a terrible noise. It was also the same time I felt an evil presence in my room when my tooth began to throb. *Was it all just happenstance?* I wondered, *or could it be something more....*

Meanwhile, I focused all my energies on praying, eating just one meal a day. Over and over I proclaimed aloud, "Thank you, Lord, that You are touching Nathan—that Your hands are surrounding him."

Three days after we had first heard about the accident, we received another phone call from George, Jr. He explained that the doctor didn't think the baby was going to make it. Soon the hospital chaplain would be talking to Charlie and Rachel to prepare them for the worst.

The next day I flew out of Haiti, arriving late at night in Boston where I stayed with George, Jr. and Paula. The following morning, I drove a rented vehicle to Albany, New York. During the two-and-a-half-hour drive, I sang songs that fueled my faith, including what would become my theme song for little Nathan, "Great and mighty is the Lord our God." I tried to recount the things I had had to trust God for in the past: my son, Timothy. Double pneumonia. The threat of breast cancer. Malaria. My own car accident. Chronic mononucleosis.

On and on the list grew. As I realized afresh how God had brought me through each crisis, my fears eased and my faith increased.

When I finally arrived at Albany Medical Center, Charlie and Rachel embraced me, their faces a mask of grief and despair. Fortunately, Nathan had been moved to the semi-intensive care unit since the medicine was beginning to control his seizures. But the doctors said there was a possibility of permanent brain damage due to the severity of his bleeding and convulsions.

"We have to trust God through this," I explained, trying to bring them some encouragement.

Rachel, who had been trained as an assistant physical therapist and had seen a lot of suffering, slowly shook her head as tears spilled from her eyes. "Yes, but these things happen to the best of people...I know that."

I visited Nathan a few minutes later, unprepared for what I saw. Barely conscious with his eyes shut, part of his skull stuck out of a swollen, misshapen head. He was hooked up to a monitor and IV. I encouraged Charlie and Rachel to get a good night's sleep while I stayed with their son.

As the minutes of the dark night ticked slowly by, Nathan often screamed out in pain. Each time he had a convulsion, my heart wrenched as I watched his little body arch and stiffen, and his eyes roll back into his head.

"Help me, Lord," I cried, "to trust You for Nathan's recovery when my natural eyes feel it's impossible. You've given me faith in the past. Give me faith for this."

Over the next few days, despite the doctor's gloomy prediction, little Nathan rallied. Soon he was fully awake and his seizures under control.

One week later, Rachel stayed by Nathan's side while he was given a MRI (Magnetic Resonance Imaging)—a brain scan that established how much damage had been done. Meanwhile, Charlie and I paced and prayed behind the closed door. Although it was a strange hospital in a strange town, the peace and presence of God were very familiar to me.

Told it would take 24 hours for the prognosis, the next day Charlie, Rachel, Nathan, and I waited in a glass-paneled room, furnished with sofas and chairs, as well as a beautiful new piano. As little Nathan rested quietly in Rachel's arms, I scooted onto the piano bench and played "Jesus Loves Me" to him. The words encouraged us during this tense time of waiting.

As we continued praising the Lord during several more hymns, the door flew open, and the doctor appeared. Searching his face for some sign of good news, I noticed a small smile playing on his lips. "From what I can tell, the MRI does not show any brain damage."

A mixture of joy and relief spread across Charlie and Rachel's faces, and my heart did a little jig. What a tremendous sense of victory we all felt.

A few days later, after Nathan was released from the hospital, I drove Charlie, Rachel, and Nathan home to Worcester. There Nathan would be cared for by a very competent Christian pediatrician. And Charlie and Rachel would also have the close support of our family and church.

On October 7, after being home for 12 days, I returned to Haiti, grateful Nathan was recovering so well.

Unfortunately, Christian efforts in Haiti—starting with our next women's meeting in November—would not end on such a happy note.

Chapter 23

Dark Valley

It was a beautiful November afternoon, and I felt very pleased. Several hundred women had attended our third interdenominational women's meeting. Not only had many of them become Christians or received personal ministry, everything had gone off without a hitch.

One hour after the meeting's conclusion, my mood darkened as a fellow missionary relayed a terrible story to me. She explained that a new missionary to the area named Wendy had planned on attending the meeting, but she had completely forgotten about it. Instead, she had filled a plastic tub of bath water for her 7-month-old baby girl, Hannah. When she had returned, Hannah was asleep on her bed. Placing the tub of water on the floor at the foot of the bed, she busied herself with housework and the care of her other three children until the baby awoke.

When she returned to check on Hannah, she discovered that her baby had fallen into the water and drowned. Devastated and alone, since her husband was in the city, she had radioed every missionary she knew of but no one was home—they were all attending our meeting.

I closed my eyes as a dull ache filled my head. The last time we had had our interdenominational women's meeting, Nathan had his accident. Then, during this one, a baby had drowned. Were they merely coincidences, I wondered, or was the enemy actively trying to discourage us, angry over the territory we were taking from him? Whatever the reason, I knew we couldn't live in constant fear and paralysis. Not only would we persevere, but we would continue to claim these women for God.

Yet more unexpected sorrow lay ahead. One of our most outstanding Haitian pastors—a key leader in the village of Ti Riviere—died a long and painful death after suffering from pneumonia and tuberculosis. Shortly after that, another one of our pastors and leader of our Bible school died of malaria and typhoid fever.

The rest of the year slipped by quickly, ushering in the new year of 1993. Despite the recent deaths of Wendy's baby and two of our pastors, the new year looked bright with promise.

On January 6, we celebrated our 10-year anniversary of NEW Missions. As I thought back over all God had done for us, I felt full of gratitude. Starting with five tents, we now had 3,500 children who were being fed and educated. And to help facilitate the large growth of our mission, George, Jr. and Paula had just moved our office to Orlando, Florida, giving us exposure to other churches and making it better suited logistically to Haiti.

I was also anticipating a momentous family event coming up in February. Mary Ann was getting married to a man named Cesar Garcia, a warm, tender-hearted man who worked in restaurant management. A large wedding was planned in Miami for our only daughter, and I wanted her day to be just right. Although I knew I had to continually surrender my children to God, often I felt I had failed Mary Ann as a mother—not being there at crucial times in her life. This time, I decided, I would make certain everything was perfect for her. I planned on making her favorite Italian cookies and buying a special coral dress for myself, one I could cherish for years to come.

In the meantime, I knew I needed to prepare for the arrival of several missionaries who would be helping us for three months. Since they had all worked with us before, I was looking forward to the renewed fellowship and extra help. Despite the fact that there were travel advisories against coming into Haiti now, and I had heard that human rights were still being violated, the atmosphere seemed fairly quiet. Apparently Cedras, who was still in office after Aristide had been ousted 15 months earlier, did whatever he deemed necessary to stay in power.

The summer heat had long since gone, replaced by a refreshing cool, but I felt sapped of vitality as I readied for my guests. Pushing down my fears of a recurrence of chronic mononucleosis, I concentrated my thoughts and energies on the coming weeks, knowing how much would be required of me. Our annual church convention was just around the corner, where thousands of people would participate in times of praise and worship and receive good Biblical training. Banners needed to be sewn, food had to be cooked and served, and arrangements made for hundreds of people to spend the weekend at our local high school and Bible school facilities.

By the time my new missionaries had arrived, however, I began experiencing a headache and chills along with fatigue. Realizing I could no longer push my body like I used to, I decided to take a couple of days off to catch my breath.

After a week, I still hadn't improved. Finally, I got some blood work done at the local hospital and was told I had malaria.

Inwardly I groaned, having had malaria at least half a dozen times before. Since I knew that malaria could eventually affect my liver and digestive system, I knew I would have to take megadoses of chloriquin to get rid of it. Unfortunately, the medication initially made me feel worse than the malaria.

However, once I took it, I usually felt better in a couple of days and back to normal in three to four weeks.

But by the time the convention began, I still hadn't improved. Again, I tested positive for malaria, requiring me to take a second dose of medication. Meanwhile, my blood pressure had plummeted, and I felt dizzy and weak. I knew I couldn't afford the luxury of lying around. I was in charge of hospitality, which meant that I had to oversee all the food and sleeping arrangements. Running on adrenaline, I attended each meeting and entertained guests throughout the long weekend.

After the convention, I managed to pass a Morse code exam in order to be licensed for the ham radio, yet I felt worse than ever. I went to the hospital for yet another blood test, which revealed that I still had malaria.

Two weeks later, I returned to the hospital for more tests. Feeling as sick as ever, I was surprised at the results: The test for malaria was now negative.

Despite the fact that I was told I no longer had malaria, I still felt too sick to even make Italian cookies for my daughter's wedding. Instead, another missionary offered to bake them for me, an offer I gratefully accepted.

On February 2, just before my daughter's wedding on the 13th, I attended our fourth interdenominational women's meeting. The church was decorated with red and pink hearts, made out of construction paper, which were strung together and fashioned into mobiles. Marching to the front, I explained to the women that I was sick but that I was trusting God to heal me.

During the meeting, Madam Robenson, a pastor's wife, was scheduled to sing for us. But she hadn't arrived yet.

Shoving my fears aside, I spoke to the women about the faithful love of Jesus, and how important it was that we didn't put our security and dependence on man. The women's heads nodded in understanding, and I knew they were encouraged, especially since many of them suffered from infidelity in their marriages.

When we had finished, I sat beside Pastor Emmanuel's wife, who was so active in serving our women. Despite the fact that she and her husband had six sons and a growing congregation, they were both deeply committed to these women's meetings. Even now, Pastor Emmanuel stood in the back, serving as a spiritual covering and making sure that the women behaved in an orderly fashion. We were also excited about our future with them. We had discussed plans for a church that would be built on the main highway where our high school and Bible school were located. The church itself would have a seating capacity of 1,500 and a team of pastors, headed by Pastor Emmanuel. Through the use of music, media, lighting, and evangelistic messages, we hoped to bring thousands of Haitians to Christ.

After the meeting was over, I discovered that Madam Robenson, who was supposed to sing, had slipped off a bridge on her bicycle on the way to our meeting. She was thrown onto rocks in the water below and was now bedridden, remaining that way for the next month.

Two days after our meeting, Pastor Emmanuel gave a young man a ride home on his bicycle after a prayer meeting, dropping him off on the side of the highway. While they were talking, a car approached. Just as the car was about to swerve to avoid hitting him, Pastor Emmanuel spotted the vehicle and jumped to the same position that the car was headed in, and was flipped onto the windshield.

Pastor Emmanuel was rushed to the hospital where he was soon greeted by George, who brought money to cover the cost of his care.

George left, feeling confident Pastor Emmanuel would make it. A few minutes later, however, he went into shock and died. An outstanding pastor and facilitator of our women's meetings was dead—the third pastor we had lost in a year.

∞ ∞ ∞ ∞ ∞

On February 10—three days before Mary Ann's wedding—George and I flew to Miami. I was now constantly plagued with digestive problems and was having severe pain on the right side of my abdomen while my stomach distended periodically. Despite how I was feeling, I was looking forward to being reunited with my family on such a happy occasion. George, Jr. and Paula would be driving in from Orlando with their 15-month-old son, Michael. Timothy, now a junior at Houghton College, would sing at the wedding. Charlie and Rachel, who were still living in West Boylston where Charlie had taken over as pastor of The Chapel, also planned on attending with 6-month-old Nathan. How anxious I was to catch up on the news concerning my grandson and to see how he was progressing. Rachel had written me, saying Nathan missed his monthly office visit in January since his pediatrician had moved. Now she was growing concerned because his head had become terribly enlarged. Since I knew that Nathan was scheduled for another appointment today, I prayed everything would go smoothly.

Mary Ann was at the airport to greet me, and we flew into each other's arms. Her long brown hair was thick and glistening, and her light brown eyes radiated an inner excitement. Not wanting to dampen her enthusiasm, I casually explained that I was sick, but that my test results said I would be feeling fine soon.

The next day, a rush of nausea overwhelmed me as Mary Ann and I searched for a coral dress for me to wear. After she accompanied me to three different malls without any success, I no longer cared. I only wanted to go home and sleep, then wake up when I was better. I settled on a light-pink linen dress that was beaded in the front. Although it was not my choice of color or fabric, the dress at least hid my distended stomach.

When we returned home, I called Charlie and Rachel in Worcester to see how Nathan's appointment had gone. Rachel explained that because of the bleeding from the accident, the ventricles in Nathan's brain were now plugged up. As a result, he required an emergency operation to put in a shunt—a tube that ran from the brain into the stomach in order to allow fluid to drain there.

The surgery was scheduled for February 16, which meant they would still attend the wedding. As a precaution, however, the doctor gave instructions for Nathan to fly with all his medical records. He then contacted a Florida hospital. The doctor also told Rachel which signs to look for that would indicate he needed emergency surgery.

I was still concerned over little Nathan and feeling miserable myself two days before the wedding, when Timothy arrived in Miami. Unfortunately, he was suffering from a mouth full of abscessed canker sores, making it impossible for him to sing. Suddenly, Mary Ann had no music for her big day.

Shortly afterwards, Charlie and Rachel flew in with Nathan. Listless and irritable, Nathan was having difficulty supporting his enlarged head.

Despite the fact that Nathan and I were sick and Timothy couldn't sing, my spirits were buoyed as the rest of the family gathered—Mom and Dad, George, Jr. and Paula and their son, Michael. What fun it was spending the night together at the Holiday Inn.

On the morning of the wedding, I took Mary Ann to get her hair done with a new beautician. As soon as we exited out the door, my daughter's face clouded with disappointment. Upset over the way her hair had turned out, she pulled out every pin, determined to fix it herself.

With only two hours remaining before the wedding, I headed back to the Holiday Inn when we became terribly lost. By the time we finally got back on track and reached our hotel, we had just one hour remaining before the limousine arrived.

Mary Ann's hair fiasco quickly faded into the background as we were faced with even more distressing news: During the night, George, Jr.'s car had been stolen from the Holiday Inn parking lot. Inside the car were his tux, video equipment, and all of the mission mail, including many checks that people had sent.

I couldn't believe it: Mary Ann's hair was a wreck, I was sick and holding my side, Nathan was preparing for emergency surgery, Timothy couldn't open his mouth, and now George, Jr. was furious over losing his car, saying he would never set foot in Miami again.

Despite our family's difficulties, the wedding, which was held in a splendid historic Spanish-style Congregational church, went off perfectly. Mary Ann looked lovely in her long, white, satin gown; her naturally wavy hair beautifully transformed from its earlier disaster, now pulled up neatly in the front while the rest flowed loosely and softly down her back. Meanwhile, her handsome, dark-haired groom stood proud and tall beside her, as his brown eyes sparkled with happiness. My two daughter-in-laws and Timothy's fiancée, Danika, lined up next to Mary Ann as her bridesmaids, while my three sons acted as the groomsmen.

Physically, though, I was barely surviving. I felt dizzy, nauseated, and weak. Yet, since friends were there whom I hadn't seen for years, I forced myself to keep going.

That evening, many of our friends and relatives left early, unwilling to stay another night at the Holiday Inn because George, Jr.'s car had been stolen from their parking lot. Charlie and Rachel had already flown back to Boston with Nathan, nervous over his tenuous condition.

Two days after the wedding, George returned to Haiti while I flew to Boston to be with Charlie and Rachel during Nathan's surgery. The operation was successful and I stayed with them several days until Nathan was able to return home.

My own condition simply wasn't improving. Not only was I still horribly weak, nauseated, and battling digestive problems, but my stomach continued to distend from time to time.

I now had insurance coverage and could go to the same hospital where I had been treated for double pneumonia. However, I knew that the doctors would run every conceivable test on me, and I felt sensitive about running up such a huge bill. Besides, maybe I really wasn't that sick— maybe I was just imagining everything. After all, the last test for malaria was negative.

I returned to Haiti and saw an American doctor there, who couldn't seem to find anything wrong. "Is there anything bothering you?" he questioned. "Any emotional stress that you're going through?"

My mind flashed back to my daughter's recent wedding and my grandson's successful surgery. "There's nothing I can think of that would make me sick. I just want to feel good."

I underwent another series of tests for malaria: This time the results were positive, making me realize that I had had malaria all along. The previous test had obviously been a false negative, which can happen if the parasite is not activating in the blood stream at the time the test is taken.

By this time I had a resistant strain of malaria—resistant to my previous medication. Unfortunately, the doctor didn't have any larium available, which was the necessary medication for treatment.

After several weeks the hospital informed me that, besides the malaria, I had two additional parasites as well.

Although one of them wasn't very serious, the other was lodged in my liver.

While the parasites were playing havoc with my body, I continued to grow sicker and sicker, rarely able to set foot out of the house. And along with my other symptoms, my temperature became uncontrollable, fluctuating between subnormal temperatures and high ones.

Here I was, a bonafide missionary and I was totally useless. I could not eat. I could not sleep.

I could do nothing.

Days passed—countless miserable, hot, sickly days. Finally, on May 1, a visiting volunteer team arrived from the States. One of them was a doctor named Linda, a southern woman in her mid-30's with short, curly hair and blue eyes. After clinic hours, she asked if she could check on me.

After detecting that my liver was enlarged, Linda gave me five larium pills, which she had taken along for herself as a precaution against malaria. I swallowed them in one large dose. Then she told me to remain in bed.

During the next few days, tortured sleep came to me only in snatches, and I constantly felt like I was going to pass out. It was decided that I should return with Linda to Miami the following morning. If I was too sick to continue on to Boston, I would remain there with Mary Ann.

On May 6, the night before our departure, I asked to speak to Linda. When she appeared, my hands tingled and I struggled to make my lips move and to make my throat push out a sound. "I feel I might...die tonight...I'm afraid I'll go into shock." My mouth felt dry, my tongue thick and heavy as I pushed my whisper a little harder: "Will you stay with me tonight in case the Lord might use you to save my life?"

Linda nodded, her face grave and serious. She had read up on tropical diseases and knew that various strains of malaria could kill a person in one day.

That night she remained close by, sleeping on our large living room couch, with immediate access to radio communication. As I lay beside George in the next room, his face was pensive, sad. "How are you feeling?"

"I can't talk now," I gasped. "I must prepare to meet the Lord."

George's eyes filled with concern, and he stroked my forehead and kissed me lightly. Then, snuggling beside me, he slowly drifted off to sleep, leaving me to face the real possibility of dying. A terrible sadness rushed over me as I thought of my family carrying on without me—my husband leading this mission alone; my children and grandchildren continuing to grow and blossom in my absence.

Yet, I was not afraid to die. Rather, I felt torn—wanting to remain with my family, yet knowing I might soon be in the glorious presence of Jesus. Over and over, I meditated on several Scriptures that I had committed to memory, such as: "In my Father's house are many mansions: if it were not so, I would have told you. I go to prepare a place for you" (John 14:2 KJV) and "Thou wilt keep him in perfect peace, whose mind is stayed on Thee" (Is. 26:3 KJV). Whatever the outcome, I felt renewed and at peace in my spirit, knowing that the hope He had put there was a hope that ultimately would never disappoint because of the outpouring of His incredible love.

Then I pictured Jesus, standing before me as I prepared to meet Him face to face.

Chapter 24

My Times Are in Thy Hands

The glow of dawn slowly invaded my room as my eyes half-opened. Feeling more dead than alive, I was nevertheless surprised that I was still here—still holding on somehow. Linda stood beside me, holding a glass of water, managing a small smile. After I took a few sips, she readied herself to go to the airport with me, along with several visitors.

George and another missionary carried me to the vehicle. They laid me on a sheet in the back seat with a pillow tucked under my head. During the slow and bumpy two-hour ride, I tried to rest as much as possible as I concentrated on making it to Miami.

At the airport, I sat on the floor, too weak to stand. One of our mission visitors handed the agent my open-ended ticket, explaining that I was sick and needed immediate medical attention stateside.

The agent stared at me as I tried to compose myself as much as possible.

Finally he shook his head. "We're sorry, but she can't go on this flight. She must have a letter from her doctor saying she can travel."

Linda, who was standing nearby, immediately wrote a note, enabling me to get on the plane. How fortunate that she was there. My mind shot back to the time when I was sick with double pneumonia and the Oriental woman had managed to get me a seat on the next plane. I shuddered. If any of the agents had discovered then how sick I was...

Once aboard, I tried to sleep while Linda diligently wrote up five pages of my medical history for the next doctor who treated me.

As soon as the plane landed, I was helped into a wheelchair. Holding my head in my hands, my body was bent over in agony. Mary Ann and Cesar—who were notified earlier of my arrival time—rushed to my side. Tears coursed down my daughter's face as she stared at me.

"I'm supposed to take a flight to Boston," I rasped.

"You're too sick," Mary Ann announced, her face taking on a determined look. "I'll take care of you."

Since my daughter was out of school and her husband wanted her to take a break before returning to work, she had time to make me a top priority. I said goodbye to Linda and was driven to the hospital to see a tropical disease specialist. Unfortunately, the specialist was away. Instead, a doctor did an ultrasound on my liver, which appeared to be fine.

Although the doctor knew I was extremely sick, he could find no concrete reason to admit me to the hospital—even my temperature was normal for a change.

After giving me an antibiotic, the doctor encouraged me to make an appointment with a tropical disease specialist in the area.

By the time Mary Ann and I saw another tropical disease specialist the following day, the antibiotic had already made me feel more nauseated and weak than I already was. My head hung between my legs as I struggled to breathe.

The woman specialist—a compassionate Vietnamese woman in her late 40's—checked me over, studied my blood results, and explained, "You definitely have malaria—and you can die from this kind at any time. I'm putting you on megadoses of flagel for 10 days for the two parasites. You'll think the medicine's killing you, but it's the only way to wipe out the parasites that are attacking your liver, digestive system, and everything else in your body." There was an urgency to her voice that set my heart pounding.

Yet, what she said next brought a special glow to my heart. "I'm a born-again believer—I believe in the laying on of hands. Can I pray for you?"

"Yes," I cried as a few tears escaped down my face, "—please lay your hands on me."

The woman nodded understandingly, then prayed that God would completely restore my health. Afterwards, the doctor, Mary Ann, and I cried together.

Just before I left, the doctor issued me a strong warning: "Never return to Haiti." She went on to explain that repeated bouts of malaria had most likely weakened my liver, and that I would be risking my health by ever going back.

During the next 10 days, I faithfully took my megadoses of flagel while I stayed at Mary Ann and Cesar's condominium. But the doctor was right: I felt like it was killing me. As my thinking became more and more muddled, my body raced out of control as though I was having a complete nervous breakdown.

Slowly, however, the medicine did its job, expelling the deadly parasites within me. After completing my required dosages, I found that I was able to keep applesauce and oatmeal down and even sit outside for short periods of time. Mary Ann also took me on scenic car rides to lift my sagging spirits. As I grew stronger, we took walks together in the park directly across the street from her condominium. What a special bond I felt between my daughter and me.

After two weeks I felt considerably better, although still very weak. Nevertheless, I decided it would be good to fly up to Worcester to be with Charlie, Rachel, and little Nathan.

Mary Ann ordered a wheelchair, and an agent wheeled me onto the airplane before the other passengers boarded. Spotting one of the stewardesses as I fell in my seat, I asked her to put my carry-on bag in the overhead compartment for me. The stewardess grudgingly obliged, then complained about it to another stewardess standing nearby, within easy ear shot of me.

As tears spilled out of my eyes, she questioned me, "What's wrong with you?"

"I'm recovering from malaria and parasites."

"I'm not sure you should be on this plane. Please step outside so we can talk."

Pushing myself up from my seat, I managed to deplane and speak with her in the lobby. "What I have is not contagious," I explained.

"How can I be sure? Are you carrying your medical papers with you?"

Nodding, I fumbled through my purse and handed them to her. After shuffling through them, she reluctantly let me board again and take my seat. A few minutes later, I wrapped myself in a blanket and curled into a ball, feeling humiliated and ashamed. How I hated being sick. For not only was I sick, but I was a sick missionary.

When I finally arrived in Boston, Charlie greeted me with a bouquet of lilacs, brightening my spirits considerably. And when we arrived at his home at Camp Woodhaven—just two doors down from the home we had lived in for so many years—there were lilacs everywhere I looked, a fragrance I had really missed in Haiti.

Over the next several days, I made a slow but steady recovery, enjoying my time with Charlie, Rachel, and Nathan, who was continuing to do well after his surgery. Then, after telling my sister Elizabeth that there were no flowers around the evergreen bushes at our father's summer camp less than a block away, she immediately brought me two boxes full of them. Each day, as I pushed Nathan in his stroller, I took several with me, praying for the strength to plant a few flowers. It was especially heart-warming to see the beautiful wooden chapel with the large glass windows standing in the distance.

Slowly, steadily, I grew stronger. Absorbing the refreshing air, I thought how good it was to be home. Since I had lived in this neighborhood for 10 years, memories came flooding back as Nathan and I passed my former home each day. I thought about the miracle of Timothy who had struggled to survive here right after he was born; the prayer time on the second floor that sparked my beginnings with Women's Aglow; the vision I had in my living room of the Indian women in their sarees. As I thought over my life, a warm glow filled my heart. How faithful God had been to us here, and afterward as we had moved into the church and eventually on to the mission field.

After being home for 10 days, I received the unexpected blessing of attending my father's 75th birthday party on May 30. Although friends and family were surprised to see me and a bit shocked by my physical appearance, it was wonderful to be with so many who had known me since childhood. Many stood and acknowledged my father in special ways, and I prayed that God would restore my health and allow me to be a strong, supportive daughter to him once again.

I was too weak to be a spiritual giant during this recovery time, but I did read biographies of women who had great faith when faced with adversity. I also continued to find encouragement in the Psalms, focusing on verses in which David persistently cried out to the Lord when he was in danger. With what little energy I could muster, I cried out to God, asking Him for renewed hope and healing. As I did, I would claim the Scripture in Isaiah 40:31 which says, "...those who hope in the Lord will renew their strength. They will soar on wings like eagles; they will run and not grow weary, they will walk and not be faint" (NIV).

Yet each time I was examined by a specialist in Worcester, I was told I still wasn't strong enough to return to Haiti. Still the days passed peacefully, restfully, as I basked in God's love and that of my family. And although it was difficult being separated from George for so long, he was able to keep in touch by ham radio every few days, easing the loneliness somewhat.

Finally, after two months, the doctor said I was well enough to return to Haiti. Before I left she admonished me to take medication regularly to prevent me from ever contracting malaria again.

On July 3, just before my departure, I received word that Haiti had signed an agreement with the United Nations. In it, the present government agreed to a democratic process, promising that Aristide would return soon to finish his term of office as president.

With Haiti's political outlook looking brighter, I flew in a few days later, throwing my arms around George, who greeted me at the airport, smiling broadly. How good it was to be reunited again with my husband. Another blessing was that Charlie, Rachel, and Nathan had agreed to return to Haiti on September 1, as full-time missionaries. While Rachel helped in the clinic, Charlie would do accounting work and city business, teach in our Bible school, and take groups by boat to do island evangelism. Not only would they be a huge asset, but I looked forward to having my grandson nearby. And there was even more good news: Rachel was expecting another baby in April.

Three and a half months later, on October 30—the day Aristide was to resume office—a ship full of security advisors and engineers was refused permission to dock at Port-au-Prince. Apparently, the agreement between Haiti and the United Nations had not been honored.

Immediately, the United Nations petitioned the rest of the world, calling for a blockade against Haiti.

Chapter 25

Whom Shall I Fear?

Mighty American naval ships cruised the waters just outside our front door. They were quite a contrast from our neighborhood village where pigs and chickens competed for a few droppings of food while a woman prepared a measly meal for too many mouths. Men clustered together, playing cards and dominoes; others sought entertainment with small talk. Their eyes appeared dull and hollow, despondent over the increased suffering they were forced to endure because of politics. It was a strange paradox: The poorest country in the western hemisphere was under a blockade, causing even more serious inflation than ever before.

For two-and-a-half years, Haiti had suffered under the embargo. Now that the gas stations were closed for more than a year, gas prices had soared to $35 a gallon on the black market, resulting in escalating prices everywhere. Apparently, gas was still bypassing the United States and coming in through another country. Fortunately, once a month, we were able to purchase gasoline directly from an agency set up by the United States for people who were doing humanitarian work. Parents complained that they no longer could afford to buy their children sneakers to wear to school since they now cost $30 dollars a pair. Even a piece of ribbon for their daughter's hair cost $2. Fortunately, we were able to get special permission from the United States government to ship two containers of lumber and mission supplies into Haiti, allowing us to continue to build another school and church.

As Americans began leaving the country, we realized that our presence was needed here more than ever. At least three times in the last three years the American embassy had sent someone to our mission, advising us to leave Haiti while it was still safe. Each time George and I shook our heads. A long time ago we had decided that if God was still calling us to Haiti, then that meant He was calling us through the good times and the bad. Besides, our hearts were here, just as the hearts were of the other missionaries who were remaining. Like us, most of them lived in rural areas among the people, developing a real bond and commitment to them.

We did take precautions, however. Although we had never advertised our mission by putting up signs, we didn't venture out now at night either. We hoped to remain secluded, ministering quietly to the 20,000 people we felt called to serve within our 8-mile radius.

George also had a plan in case of an unexpected attack from thieves or political groups. Since hundreds of green army blankets had been donated to our mission, he made sure that each of us received one. Then George explained that if he ever gave a sharp yell, we were to immediately flee to the sugarcane fields with our blankets—which would help camouflage and protect us from insects and chill—and hide.

As the political situation intensified, 25 Haitian men started watching through the night, making sure no one tried to steal food from our warehouse. They also placed coconut logs across our roads at various locations to discourage unwanted visitors.

Meanwhile, President Clinton, Jean-Bertrand Aristide, and Robert Malval, the current prime minister of Haiti, met, trying to reach a compromise with the military leaders here.

They appeared to be hopeful that a settlement would be reached before Christmas.

Each Friday night, we invited missionaries from all over the Leogane Plain to come together for a time of fellowship and teaching. During these dark political days, many shared information they had received. Depending on the person who shared, it would either reinforce our fear or our faith. One night, a woman related how five Haitian men in her area had stolen a vehicle that was owned by an agency in the country. After the police found out who had stolen it, they had captured the men, never bothering to try them or to bring them to the police station. Instead they had their bodies cut up and strewn in a public place. Apparently, the present government was encouraging these extreme punishments as a way to instill fear.

As frightening as these stories were, I knew I couldn't allow my imagination to run wild, living in fear and letting it intimidate me. I felt like David when he cried out in Psalm 27:1 "Whom shall I fear? Of whom shall I be afraid?" Although we were all tired from the unknown and the injustices that were taking place, I knew without a shadow of a doubt that God had called us here. As a result, I felt safe in knowing there was no more secure a place than to be living in the center of His will. Besides, here at NEW Missions, we were surrounded by people who loved us and wanted us here. Also, because the officers in charge of the police and the military had told their men that no Americans were to be touched, we were treated with the utmost courtesy.

As Christmas came and went with no word of a settlement, Charlie and Rachel flew back to South Carolina to await the birth of their second child. Meanwhile, I could see the pain on the Haitians' faces as they gathered in our churches each Sunday and prayed. One of their favorite songs was: "There He is...He's coming. There He is...He's coming. I'll see Him face to face...." For now, the Haitian people felt as though the nations of the world had deserted them, and they were resolved to live alone in a never-ending state of misery.

As the Haitians' suffering increased, so did my sensitivity. Memories of my illnesses and pain led me often to the clinic, to comfort and encourage the sick and the dying. I also tried to do my best to make sure that a Haitian baby had the same medicine and help that my grandson had received—whether it was amoxicillin for an ear infection or a shunt for his head.

In November, just such a need occurred.

Her name was Naomi and she was 9 months old. When she was born, her umbilical cord had been cut with an unsterile household knife, resulting in a severe infection. Now, Naomi had developed water on the brain and required a shunt. Yet, after we had sent her to three different hospitals, the embargo had prevented the doctors from having the necessary materials to perform the operation. Besides that, doctors were now scarce since many of them had also fled.

Soon I was praying and fasting for Naomi, trying to figure out a way to save her life. Then I discovered that, through the Rotary Club, I might be able to get Naomi to the States.

One afternoon, as I was praying on the clinic floor next to Naomi and her mother, a middle-aged doctor entered the room. Since I was in need of a doctor's recommendation for Naomi before the Rotary Club would accept her, I asked him to take a look at her.

The doctor peered at Naomi from behind thick glasses as she lay listlessly beside me—her head enlarged from all the fluid on her brain. Then, scooping her up in his arms, he did a quick examination.

Afterwards, the doctor turned to me and announced, "Don't spend a penny on this child. She needs a shunt, but she's got other problems too."

My mind reeled from his words, for I understood all too well what his underlining thoughts were: Why spend money to save someone this sick when the money could be used helping more people who weren't as critical?

I thought of my American grandson, who had received the very best medical attention. Yet, since Naomi had been born to a poor Haitian mother, the mighty dollar decided her fate.

I stared back at the doctor confidently, stubbornly. "When you have grandchildren," I explained boldly, "you'll find it more difficult to say something like that."

The doctor's face was expressionless as he turned and left without a word, unwilling to give Naomi the written recommendation she required. I turned to Naomi's mother, whom I knew was dreaming of sending her baby to the States. "The doctor doesn't give us much hope, but God has the final word. In the meantime, we'll knock on every door we can."

∞ ∞ ∞ ∞ ∞

On April 5, I found out by ham radio that Rachel had given birth just 30 minutes earlier to another baby boy, Jeremie John. I also looked forward to welcoming a new daughter-in-law into our family. Timothy, who would be completing his college degree in communication in May, had recently announced he and Danika would be married May 28, 1994.

Meanwhile, although political negotiations appeared to be at a stalemate, Aristide wanted the United Nations to tighten the embargo to hasten his return to Haiti. Not only were the military, parliament, and the upper class opposed to his returning, but the Haitian people in general were tired— tired of the loss of jobs and the skyrocketing prices in their country. However, the consensus of opinion seemed to be that things would remain pretty much the same until Aristide's 5-year term ran out, which wouldn't be for another 20 months.

By May, the United States decided to put even more pressure on the present government: Starting June 24, no planes were allowed to fly in or out of Haiti to or from the United States. This meant that thousands of Haitians who lived in the United States and visited Haiti to bring gifts to their families could no longer do so. It also meant that porters and taxi drivers could no longer earn an adequate living, and that visitors, who generated money through the departure tax, would no longer be helping the economy either. Since the rich and those in power always found a way around the measures of the embargo, I realized this new restriction would only add to the suffering of the poor.

Now the last crumbs that remained were going to be taken away.

Before the planes stopped flying, we flew to the States to attend Timothy's college graduation. Two weeks later, he and Danika were married in a lovely wedding ceremony. George performed the ceremony and Timothy sang a song he composed to his bride. A few days later, George and I flew to Haiti, anxious to return while we still could.

Meanwhile, there was a mass exodus of Americans, leaving only a small number remaining in Haiti. Although we were told that 75 percent of all missionaries had now left Haiti, George and I still felt we should stay. How could we proclaim that our hope and security was in Christ, and that we shouldn't be dismayed or fearful if we fled the country every time things got bad? How could we be effective if we weren't willing to help these people during the tough times as well as the good?

We likened it to a marriage—and we were in it for better or worse. Had God called us to Haiti only when the sun was brightly shining? No, we decided. Besides, the darker it got, we knew that the brighter the light of Jesus would shine.

Our biggest concern, however, was for 2-year-old Nathan, who would return to Haiti with his parents and baby brother, Jeremie, before the planes stopped flying. If Nathan developed an infection and didn't have immediate medical attention, critical complications could develop.

We knew, however, that being in the United States did not always promise complete protection. After Nathan's car accident, Charlie and Rachel became friends with a couple who had an 11-year-old daughter who also had a shunt. Recently, she had developed an infection and died in the middle of the night in one of the best medical facilities. In memory of their daughter, the parents had encouraged people to send money to our mission clinic.

On June 1, Charlie and Rachel flew to Haiti, feeling their place was here. Three other missionaries decided to remain with us as well.

Charlie resumed his ministry to the fishermen, starting a Sunday school class for them. As 60 men joined him— including the local police—Rachel greeted them with two large pots of tea loaded with sugar and milk. Many of them eventually had conversion experiences. As for the rest of us, instead of sitting around listening to the doom and gloom of the newscasts, we decided to have a huge church revival. To prepare us for whatever was going to take place, we wanted to ignite the fire of the Holy Spirit in each of our lives. Night after night, after decorating the church with colorful balloons, we were packed to capacity as the Haitians prayed, worshipped, and looked to God for their hope and deliverance. Their extreme misery fired an intense hope in God.

In mid-June, a pastor from Louisiana decided to fly into Haiti with a group of 27 to do volunteer work at our mission for a week. Despite tremendous opposition from family and church members, the group arrived in Haiti as local news media covered the event. Loaded with canned foods and other supplies, their supplies would turn out to be a real help to us in the months to come.

One week later, the group left on one of the last flights out of Haiti. Then, on June 24, American planes stopped flying. Now the only commercial flights in and out of Haiti were with Air France. To get to the United States, we would have to travel by way of another country, such as the Dominican Republic.

Throughout the summer, a few remaining missionaries in our area joined us every Friday evening. One of the doctors who attended continually admonished Rachel to leave Haiti with her two children. Women and children from five other missions in our surrounding area had all left. The doctor's own wife had also left, and he felt it was foolish for Rachel to remain here any longer, especially with Nathan's physical condition. Rachel continued to remain adamant. They were staying. Charlie and Rachel still felt their place was here; therefore, that meant putting their trust in God and committing little Nathan's life into His hands as well.

Despite the turmoil around us, the mission continued to flourish, a testimony to God's faithfulness and goodness. We had 180 Haitian employees, our tanks were full of gas, our warehouse was full of food, and our clinic—which was staffed with 25 people and cared for 20,000 people—was still filled with the best medicines available. We also had 550 women in our prenatal program.

But I was troubled. Over and over I kept hearing stories of people with typhoid fever or malaria who went to their own medicine men instead of to our clinic. These medicine men put leaves and leeches over the sick person's body, supposedly to suck off the bad blood. Or the people sometimes went to their voodoo priests who made them appease some angry spirit by forcing them to sell their meager possessions. In the end, they usually died.

I decided to invite all the medicine men and voodoo priests to our clinic. On the big day, after having our Haitian women make hundreds of chocolate cupcakes, 70 people gathered, several who were doctors from two health agencies. Their goal was to introduce alternative medical care to the people.

I opened the meeting and scanned the crowd of voodoo priests, medicine men, Haitian midwives, and doctors. I felt intimidated. Silently, I cried out to God.

Immediately I heard His still, small voice, encouraging me to preach the Gospel.

Opening my Creole Bible, I took the opportunity to share for a few minutes from the book of Jeremiah. As I spoke about God's power and presence during these difficult times in Haiti, His sweet presence seemed to permeate the room.

One of the voodoo priests—an elderly man dressed in a baggy gray suit—stood up. "I see children coming home from this mission, and they're given food and money," he explained. "The good God sent the mission here to do what we couldn't do for our own people."

Then another voodoo priest rose: "My grandfather and father were both voodoo priests." Pausing, he lowered his eyes: "I don't know how to do anything else." Then he apologized and sat back down.

Then another stood and explained: "I want to be in church every Sunday. It will be hard to walk down the road, knowing that children will taunt me for attending. But I want to come and be a part of you."

By the time our meeting had ended, and the medicine men and voodoo priests had received spiritual as well as practical help, I realized that the chains of voodoo were slowly beginning to loosen.

Not only were our relationships strengthening with the medicine men and voodoo priests, but so were our relationships with the rest of the villagers. By remaining in Haiti during this tense time, we were proving our commitment to them. This caused our words to carry even more weight.

Yet, outside of our surrounding area, we rarely felt welcome anymore. Instead, I could sense the anger mounting against those of us who were Americans. We became the enemy—the reason for their economic suffering.

Soon came word that a United States intervention would take place, causing us even more uncertainty. The one thing Haitians were united in was their opposition to foreign occupancy. After being ruled by France and gaining their independence in 1804, the Haitians still prided themselves on being the first free black republic in the world—and they had no intention of ever being ruled again.

Democracy seemed impossible for another reason. No democratic institutions existed in Haiti; the infrastructure had deteriorated to almost nothing, and there was only a small middle class with a huge chasm between the rich and the poor. Without the support of the leadership that now controlled Haiti—which were the elite, the business community, and the military—democracy could never be realized. I knew that the Haitians would see Americans as a scapegoat and the source of their problems.

As a result, the forces in power now threatened to fight until the end. Certainly their philosophy in the past, when gaining their first independence, was to kill every Frenchman and burn every home. *Would history repeat itself*, I wondered, *as they tried to kill every American in Haiti?*

I had to ask myself, *who would fight? What if some of our high school students ended up fighting American soldiers? How would I feel if our American soldiers were forced to kill the youth I had worked with for 12 years?*

So many hopes and fears crowded into my mind. Why couldn't the United States just let Haiti take care of its own problems? It was futile, I realized, to try and export democracy—it had to be in the minds of the people to be successful. If the government didn't understand democracy, they would never understand compromise. As a result, it might take a whole new generation to make that happen.

At the same time, although no one in Haiti wanted to see an American intervention, the Haitians were so worn down—so oppressed by the corruption of those in office—that many were beginning to believe the intervention might be a tool of God's deliverance for them.

While the intervention was set to take place, an 81-year-old man—chief of all the voodoo priests and illegally elected as president—called for the highest sacrifices of voodoo to be performed for 30 days to try and prevent the Americans from taking control. As soon as I heard the news, I shuddered. The highest sacrifice of voodoo, it was rumored, involved children. Those of us who were Christians instead prayed and fasted for a peaceful intervention.

On October 3, during the late hours of the night, the skies filled with helicopters and huge transport planes which flew over our mission thundering frightening noise on their way to the airport, dropping off troops and supplies. Aircraft carriers, destroyers, cruisers, and a hospital ship filled our waters.

Soon word reached us that American tanks were lining up in front of F.R.A.P.H. (Front for the Advancement and Progress of Haiti), a paramilitary organization that tyrannized the Haitian people. One hundred and fifteen leaders of F.R.A.P.H. were arrested and more than 4,000 weapons confiscated.

I thought of the small children running into the open fields, awakened by the screaming skies, without lamps or any way to see. They must be terrified, I realized, wondering if the planes were coming to kill them or to bring them food.

Throughout the night, we prayed and waited in tense silence.

Soon God answered our prayers for a peaceful intervention. Within the next several weeks, as Americans occupied the country, Cedras stepped down and left the country without incident.

Soon I ventured into the city, noticing that the streets were still a noisy blend of honking cars and merchants hawking their wares, maintaining an outward appearance of normalcy. However, it was strange now seeing American soldiers dressed in heavy combat gear, wearing bulletproof vests, their faces sweating from the hot Haitian sun.

I walked up to one young American and said, "God be with you. You're here on orders and so am I. It could cost us our lives. We both have a very high calling."

The soldier smiled and nodded as I turned on my heels and carried on with my shopping. For the first time in several years, I finally felt safe to move about the country. And in just a few months, the United Nations planned to take over the responsibilities of security, as well as help with other development projects. The politicians would finally be free to try and establish a new government as cabinet members and department heads were put in place. Meanwhile, Jean-Bertrand Aristide had returned as president, giving the Haitians the opportunity to bring democracy to their country.

Yet, just when things seemed to be settling down in Haiti, a tropical storm was brewing, threatening to destroy our very community.

Chapter 26

Hope for Tomorrow

It was Saturday afternoon, November 14, as I gazed outside, watching the rain beat down against my window. Although the rainy season should have been over by now, it continued to pour down relentlessly throughout the day.

The next day it was still raining hard and I was becoming concerned. The whole courtyard of our community house had filled with water and the level was steadily rising. I took in my surroundings, and I felt a twinge of apprehension. Two major rivers sat to the right and left of us, and I was concerned that their waters could eventually jump their banks.

I tried to take comfort in the fact that if we were in real danger, someone would have notified us on the radio. However, even as the rain poured down unmercifully, the radio remained silent. There was nothing even on the Haitian news.

Then, at 9:00 P.M., one of our missionaries came running over to our home. "We're being flooded," he yelled. "Our storage depots and community house are full of water!"

Wasting no time, George had our missionaries take shelter at our mission training center, which was situated on higher ground.

After the missionaries were settled, George and I grew more concerned about our own home, which was built on a concrete slab, just six inches up from the ground. As we examined the water level outside, we realized we had just one more inch to go before it finally flowed into our home.

As the night wore on, however, the rain seemed to be subsiding somewhat. Finally, I fell into a deep sleep.

At 1:30 A.M., I was awakened by someone pounding at our door. George sprang to his feet and opened it. Rubbing my eyes from sleep, I noticed it was one of our high school boys from Neply, now sick and trembling with fever. With his family standing behind him, he explained that the voodoo priest—one of their relatives—had smeared an ointment all over his body and head, making him feel even sicker. Finally he had told his family to take him to Pastor George.

There was another, even more pressing reason why they were there: Neply was being severely flooded. Already the water had risen to people's knees.

I stumbled out of bed and made them tea, putting out every available cookie I could find. George put the boy in the shower, along with some shampoo and soap, to wash the foul-smelling ointment off of him. George rummaged through his clothes and handed him a shirt and a fresh pair of pants.

After the family had some tea and cookies, George took them to a spare room at our mission training center, where our missionaries were staying. There they could all spend the night safely.

That was just the beginning, however. Soon we were besieged by people flocking to our mission, screaming and crying as they held children and personal belongings in their arms. In the black of night, water rose quickly in their homes, carrying away everything in its path. There were no flashlights. No lanterns. Only the terrifying sensation of water overtaking everything they owned.

George had the church opened and blankets passed out so that the Haitians could take refuge for the night. There they slept on pews while others slept outside on the clinic's deck, which was dry and on higher ground.

Sleep eluded me the rest of the night as I tossed and turned, my mind on the plight of the Haitians. *What would we find in the morning?* I wondered. *How many homes and lives would be lost?*

As soon as dawn broke, we were informed that we had been hit by a tropical storm system in our area—Storm Gordon. Wanting to survey the damage for myself, I walked towards Bord Mer but found myself immediately immersed mid-ankle in mud. My eyes scanned our school rooms, where I noticed George, shaking his head. He had just had every one of our school buildings completely repainted, inside and out. Now they were caked in two to three feet of mud.

Next, my eyes fastened onto our main road which led to the highway. Even from my vantage point, it was obvious that it was completely impassable, layered in mud and water with three large separations in it.

Realizing the mud I was in was probably swirling with raw sewage of humans and animals, I hurried home, deciding it wasn't worth the risk to my health. Once there, I threw bleach all over my body, then washed myself thoroughly with fresh water, making sure I didn't pick up any parasites.

Soon reports from the surrounding villages poured in. Many of the people in Neply, who hadn't camped out at our church, had managed to find refuge in houses of friends or relatives on higher ground. Fortunately, there was no loss of life.

The village of Masson, just three miles from our mission, was a different matter. There a river had jumped its banks and found the path of least resistance—a road that ran right through the center of the village, next to our own school and church building. Unlike Neply, there was no warning; the water did not rise slowly. Instead, five feet of

water rushed down the road at midnight, destroying everything in its sight and sweeping literally hundreds of mothers,
fathers, and children out into the ocean.

One pastor had been instrumental in saving four children who ran into our Masson church for safety. Connected
to the church were several classrooms and two smaller
rooms where the pastor lived. Grabbing the children, the
pastor took them to one of his rooms and lifted them up onto
the rafters, seating them on two wooden doors he had stored
there. Moments later, the water burst into the church building, carrying it away. Fortunately, the church helped
decrease the force of the river, so that the classrooms and
small room where the pastor and children had taken refuge
remained standing.

My mind spun over the tremendous needs that awaited
us. Unlike the United States, Haiti had no special disaster
relief agency that we could call for help. Yet, we were in no
position to help ourselves. Because of the embargo, we had-
n't had American visitors for months. This meant we had no
storeroom of gifts. And now with the intervention going on,
certainly no one planned on visiting any time soon.

The days flew by as we found ourselves caught in a
whirlwind of activity, trying to meet needs. After visiting the
U.S.A.I.D. agency to ask for assistance, I was informed that
they couldn't help us. We were left to do what we could.
Four to five feet of mud covered the school rooms in
Masson. Three of our pastors lost all of their belongings.
Children came to school, having lost their books, uniforms,
ID cards, and shoes. The hardest part was seeing children
who had lost one or both of their parents. Doing what we
could, we gave each of our students a sack of food, a gallon
of oil, and a gift of money.

The cleaning job was enormous. George directed our
missionaries to oversee several crews who worked with
shovels, hoes, brushes, soap, and pressure hoses to clean up

our classrooms and walkways. He also had a crew begin immediate work on our dirt roads, first using a tractor and blade, and then using hoes to help take off the remaining mud. Later, they spread new gravel.

The next day, we bid goodbye as people slowly vacated our church building. Many of them returned to live with relatives in already overcrowded conditions. Then George chose a group of the more intelligent Haitian high school students he knew and took them to the river banks. There he showed them where some of the farmers had cut into the bank so that water would flow into their land to irrigate it. The danger was that if the waters rose again, the river could once again break through the parts where it had been cut. Hopefully, this discouraged the Haitians from cutting any further.

A few weeks later, I attended our annual church convention where all of our NEW Mission churches and others in our surrounding area had gathered together. My ears perked up as I listened to the drums beating in the distance, played by our high school students along with our new instrumental band. How things had changed since George and I had first arrived. Back then, it was the voodoo drums calling the people. Now our drums were calling the Haitians to worship.

As I stood near the back, George invited Captain John Silkman, an American commander who was sitting with several of his men, to come to the platform and give a word of encouragement. Tall with angular features and steel blue eyes, Captain Silkman strode to the front. After greeting everyone, he explained that he wanted to serve the Haitians and be part of the new Haiti.

As Captain Silkman sat down a few minutes later, however, the ache in my soul reached deeper than ever in light of the new calamity that had befallen our people. Many had lost even the meager possessions they owned in the storm. And recently, I was informed that baby Naomi, who had desperately needed a shunt and other medical attention, had died the day Storm Gordon had hit.

Yet, as we clapped and sang about God's deliverance and our hope and trust in Him, I noticed something quiet and bold shining through the Haitians' faces. There was no bitterness, no questioning or anger toward God, only a willingness to embrace their new suffering and move on.

My eyes fixed on the young Haitian men and women who were leading us—men and women who were saved by our first wave of missionaries when they were just 10 years old, the same ones who had followed Cindy around when she had made hut calls. Now, in the face of crippling poverty and political upheaval, they stood like strong cedar trees during a great storm, their hope and security strongly fixed in God.

A warm glow swept over me as I thought of all the miracles that were represented in the lives of the Haitians here. I watched as Yolene sang a solo, her voice a soothing beacon amidst this latest challenge. As her face shone with an inner radiance, it was hard to believe that Satan had once ruled her life. Then there was pretty, petite Vania, another high school student. When Vania had become a Christian as a young teenager, her father—one of the voodoo priests— had completely disowned her, saying the only thing he would ever provide for her was a coffin for her grave. Yet, by looking at her joyful countenance now, no one would ever know the rejection she had suffered as a result of her Christian faith.

My own sponsored child, Manise, who stood with her boyfriend in the aisle next to me, was in her second year of high school. I could still remember the picture George had of her as an 8-year-old—her orange hair, flaky skin and dull, sunken eyes, all signs of severe malnutrition. It was hard to believe that the lovely young woman who stood near me, so vibrant and full of life, was once that same little girl.

Scanning the room, my eyes shifted to 13-year-old Myrtha as she placed her hands on the heads of two young girls and prayed for them. I remembered when she was 2 years old and very sick. The large family of nine had exhausted their resources and had no money for doctors or medicine, so they had put her in a box outside to die. Unexpectedly, a relative came by to visit and provided help for the child. Today, the entire family is serving the Lord and are some of the most faithful members of our mission.

Ten-year-old Judy, whom Kelli named after loosening her umbilical cord that was wrapped twice around her neck, was now a bright, bubbly child in our school. Next to her stood 9-year-old Gims whose cord I had cut as a baby. Often I reminded them that God had special plans for their lives. Nearby stood 8-year-old Jezila who was thrust in my arms as a baby, near death. After Yvette had nursed her back to health, she had become a sweet, timid child who loved Jesus. Often I reminded her of how God had used Yvette to save her, and that He had special purposes for her life.

Jezila's mother, Olimcia, stood next to her, along with her other six children. After the deaths of Edna and Olimcia's husband, we had raised money among our missionaries to help her build a cement home. Olimcia's face was far more relaxed these days, especially since her children were all being fed and educated in our school system.

Although Rodrigues was no longer with us—having died as a 10-year-old soon after we had arrived in Haiti—his brother, Michelet, stood nearby. How ironic it was that Michelet was now excelling in high school in his place, after stripping Rodrigues of his uniform after he had died.

On and on the stories went as my eyes swept around the room—stories of God's faithfulness to a people that the rest of the world had given up on. But it was the Haitians themselves—their stubborn hope in the midst of impossible odds—that suddenly broke me.

Dropping my head between my knees, my shoulders heaved up and down as tears burst from my eyes. *Lord, I* sobbed silently, *I'm not worthy to even give up my life for these beautiful people.* At times in the past, I had struggled with loneliness, sickness, and constant political upheaval. Now, for the first time, I realized I could no longer measure up to the people I served. For they had learned what it meant to rejoice and persevere in their sufferings. They had discovered a hope that would never disappoint them, a hope that God had poured into their hearts by the Holy Spirit because of His great love.

All my life, I had had a deep yearning for God to use me in whatever way He chose. Yet, these people were living out lives of faith, suffering, perseverance, and trust to a greater degree than I had ever done. They were examples of holding on when things got tough, to "keep-a-going" as my grandmother used to say, in the face of overwhelming circumstances. Through them, I realized that God wanted to use each of us, even through difficulties and hardships, if we were willing to persevere and put our hope and trust in Him. Only then would we have the strength and grace to face whatever circumstances we found ourselves in; only then would we experience a hope that would never disappoint us.

Brushing a few tears away, I saw the dream that George and I had for this "New Generation" was becoming a reality. Our dream wasn't simply to build 10 schools and have an enrollment of 4,000 well-fed and educated students. It wasn't just to increase the quality of educational facilities, or start a business school, which would teach the Haitians administrative skills, allowing them greater employment opportunities in their country. Nor was it simply to branch out into satellite schools and churches, assisting those who already had a building, yet still needed additional funds to hire pastors, teachers, and buy materials.

No, our real dream was for the Holy Spirit to blow upon this new generation of Haitians and call them to the mountains, cities, and islands of their country to become a light to their people. And now, some of our young people were doing just that. Those who had graduated from our schools were already dispersing, building their own churches and schools and becoming teachers, preachers, and administrators at our mission and throughout Haiti.

As I gazed through red-rimmed eyes at the faces throughout that simple church, I saw the leaders of tomorrow—the hope of Haiti.

I was without disappointment. I saw the "New Generation."

If you would like to correspond with Jeanne DeTellis personally or obtain more information regarding short-term mission opportunities or how to sponsor a child, please write to:

NEW Missions
P.O. Box 2727
Orlando, FL 32802

or e-mail:

jeanne@newmissions.org

or call:

(407) 240-4058

You can also visit our web site at:

http://www.newmissions.org